Advance Reviews

Published by:

SID Publishing

42 Bardeen Ct

Towson, MD 21204

www.SidMcNairy.com

Copyright (c) 2017 Sid McNary

978-0-9975383-1-1 hardback

978-0-9975383-4-2 Kindle ebook

978-0-9975383-3-5 paperback

Library of Congress Control Number: 2017914450

Cover Photograph by Kerry Brett

Cover design by www.ThisIsFour.com

Interior design by MediaNeighbours.com

Printed in the United States

Notice

The information in this book is meant to supplement not replace proper athletic, yogic, therapeutic, meditation, or fitness training. Like any training there may be some risk. The author and publisher advise readers to take full responsibility for their safety and know their limits. Before undertaking any part of this book, be sure to have consulted with your physician or healthcare provider to confirm that you are physically capable of participation in such activities without injury. Before practicing the skills described in this book be sure you do not take risk beyond your level of experience, aptitude, training, and comfort zone.

This book is dedicated to the Supreme Father, to the Supreme Mother, and to the world and to creating peace in your life for all the days to come.

Contents

Foreword

I consider it an honor and privilege to have been chosen to pen the foreword for this courageous work, expressed and articulated through my friend and brother, Sid. Whether you picked up this book as an interesting and entertaining read into the life of a successful yogi, with genuine curiosity about what a Nahi Warrior truly is, or as an investigative peek into ideas that may assist in your personal quest for inner peace, *The Warrior Within* offers insights, stories, and allegories that will intrigue, stimulate, and elevate your way of looking at and understanding life.

Part One begins with a beautiful prayer and moves eloquently through the Four Cornerstones of birthing the Nahi Warrior inside, your Champion Warrior within. Citing the details of his own personal story, Sid weaves his triumphs, failures, and life lessons to illustrate how he came to understand and realize his purpose. He has an uncanny ability to remember details of his life and recall situations and circumstances with such clarity and exactness that he takes you directly into the scene he describes to pull you in and enhance the lesson and meaning of the experience.

The Four Cornerstones move you through the process of self-awareness to release the guilt and shame of victim consciousness, and to understand the effects of science. As you start to understand "how it all works," you are invited into the flow of all the good that surrounds us, if we would but recognize that it is there.

Sid's personal quest for transformation and realization has led him to the four corners of the Earth and has exposed him to a plethora of spiritual teachings and traditions. His Native American heritage, Christian training, and open-mindedness, have allowed him to discover insights and ideas that challenge traditional, common beliefs. The discoveries he shares in the pages of this work open him up to criticism and skepticism, but they further demonstrate his conviction to the truth.

As he begins the transition into Part Two, we are introduced to the last of the Four Cornerstones. It may be the most significant of them all, the importance of practice. Specifically, Sid emphasizes remaining open to the importance of practice and the benefits realized by doing so.

In Part Two, we are guided through this thing called life, using an analogy of sports. I met Sid at Purdue University as a young coach. We were both interested in achievement and staying open to God's call and direction for our lives. He volunteered to help as I was thrust into a full-time position that most would argue I wasn't prepared for. The Bible offers that the iron sharpens iron, and that is what happened. We challenged each other and helped each other, and a bond was formed, or possibly remembered.

The Spirit of the Game includes the virtues of faith, heart, love, and wisdom. It shares wonderful stories and illustrations of how these qualities are realized and recognized in life. If you are a seeker of truth, an aspiring yogi on the path, a player recently released, or a coach looking for inspiration, I am thankful you have been led to this work. Read it with an open mind. Read it with an open heart. There is wisdom here. There is love here. Peace is here.

Peace and blessings,
Rick Smith
Executive Vice President and General Manager,
the Houston Texans

Acknowledgements

As I finish this book, I sit here in West Palm Beach, Florida, enjoying the sunrise of this beautiful day. Right in this moment, I am blessed to use this day that has never been used before. I am here getting ready to send my son, TD, off to college. I must first thank great spirit, the almighty creator of all, for this life. Father and Mother, you have allowed me to breathe, and my words cannot come close to the gratitude that I have in my heart in every day and in every moment. Thank you for this life.

My life has had many twists and turns. Through all of it, there have been several people who have made huge impacts along the way. To everyone I have ever crossed paths with, I am truly grateful. The information and wisdom from this book comes from the peace I have discovered through this life. My personal quest for peace has shaped each and every page of *The Warrior Within: A Quest for Peace*, and I am extremely excited for everyone who finds this book in their hands, for each page turned will begin to unfold a journey within to find peace in every way. It has truly been a blessed journey to have had teachers show up in many forms through this beautiful thing we call life.

In this moment, I am grateful to have this opportunity to thank everyone who has come into my life. No matter how long or short, meeting everyone has been a blessing. My mother and father, Mrs. Bobbie McNairy and Dr. Sidney A. McNairy Jr., thank you for giving me such a great life that has not only given me an amazing foundation but also allowed me to move forward as a strong man in every way possible. Thank you to the lineage of those before me, whose shoulders I stand on. Your sacrifices along the way are why I am able to do what I do today, and for that, I am eternally grateful.

To my sister Alicia and brothers David and Steve, thank you for being real in every way. The many laughs we have shared for so long have been incredible. Thank you for your support and especially for celebrating all of the victories along the way. To my nieces and nephews, thank you for smiling and being a spark that allows me to see a better day through your eyes. Brittany, thank you for coming into my life and blessing our family with love. You are a beautiful reflection of your mother.

To my kids, I say thank you. Thank you for being the ones to show me my true reflection. Thank you for allowing me to see the man I am today and how to be happy with the man I see when I look in the mirror. Camille, the beautiful woman you have grown up to be has elevated me in so many ways. Thank you for blessing my life. To "TD," Trent David, thank you for being yourself. The person you were, are, and will be has challenged me to be a better human being. Your desire to be the best version of you possible has challenged me from day one to be the best example you deserve in a father. Sid IV, the desire you have to walk in my footsteps has helped me to continue to move forward every day so you would continue to have something to reach for. May all of you continue to shine bright, and know that everyone who gets to meet you is blessed to have done so.

Rick Smith, my man. My ace for many moments now. You and I have had the pleasure of moving through the football world together, then walk on a spiritual path together, even when we were not aware of it, and I am grateful to share life with you. There have been many times when our conversations have lead to shifts either mentally, spiritually, or physically. I am grateful for our many life moments that continue to move me forward to a more powerful spirit in every way. Your friendship has been one of life's greatest treasures, and I am eternally grateful. Our friendship has stood through the test of time, and that is nothing short of magnificent. Our paths move through many turns and transformations, and it brings peace to my heart to know I can count on you in any moment that comes my way.

To the many coaches I have had the pleasure of spending time on the field with, I am grateful. Thank you to those I played for, those I coached with, and those I coached against; you all have been the ones to awaken the competitive spirit that allows me to reach for my highest self in every way. Special thanks to Coach Stevens and Coach Bichy, my childhood soccer coaches. Coach Harvill, Coach Joyce, Coach Perry, Coach Kephart, Coach Spoo, Coach Holms, Coach Novak, Coach Melvin, Coach Skerry, and Coach Mitchell, thank you for the opportunity to learn and grow in your presence.

Deon Mitchell, Darrell Hill, Justin McCareins, and PJ Fleck, my daughter's godfathers and my players with whom I have many memories, thank you. The camaraderie we shared in a game we all love has shaped my life in more ways than may ever be known. Thank you for the teacher/ student relationship. The coach/ player relationship is only as good as those involved in the relationship. Thank you all for being incredible. Because of your desire to achieve greatness, you all pulled me to a higher place within. Thank you for allowing me to coach.

To the many healers, teachers, and mentors, thank you for your care and love along the way. Because of your willingness to give, I stand here today, powerfully ready to continue to touch lives as you have my own life. What could be said about each of you is a book in and of itself. Thank you for the impact you have had on my life. A special thanks to Grandmother Morning Star, Baron Baptiste, and Rodney Yee, as your interactions with me have helped me move along this journey as a powerful spiritual teacher.

I have had the pleasure to work with some amazingly talented photographers over the years. Your images have aided in keeping memories alive in my head, so that many stories could be told. A special thanks to Harry Dezitter, Seth Shimkonis, Amy Hefter, Karen L. Messick, and many more. Your work has captured moments like no other. To Kerry Brett, thank you for capturing this cover and the soul of a man who has lived the quest for peace.

Elyssa Williams, thank you for your efforts. Your desire to help bring forward the story to share peace, so the world may have it, has been a great blessing. I look forward to all that will come forward for you and all who are able to take part in this journey. Thank you for the many hours you dedicated to moving this forward.

To my fellow yoga teachers, thank you for doing what you do. The world is a better place because of what you do. No matter what style you teach or where you teach, everyone has an opportunity to shift in your presence. To Patty Ivey, Kiersten Mooney, Amanda Shields, Kelly Dunaja, and Crystal Wesner, please know how grateful I am to call you all my friends. Thank you for standing with me through this journey, and know I am here for you any time. I am always just a phone call away.

To the thousands of people I have had an opportunity to teach and be inspired by, I say thank you. May your lives continue to be blessed as you have blessed mine. Until our eyes meet again, be blessed.

To Liz Hahn, I saved this for last because there are so many amazing things to say. You have stood for me in ways that are like no other. Your ability to love me has taught me to love all, free of conditions. Thank you for all of your support. Everything happens for a reason, and that moment we were left in the water together was the start of this amazing journey. Thank you for allowing me to see and know all of you, as your beauty is all I can see, the true you—love at its finest. Thank you for being love and reflecting it back tenfold. You have allowed me to soften, love myself more deeply, remove all the wounds from my heart, and for that I will spend many, many moons letting you know how special you are to me. Thank you, my love, for being my split-apart. I have found it, and it is in you! I love you to the moon and back. Thank you for sharing this life with me.

For all of the amazing people I have not mentioned, know that you have a space in my heart. I love and appreciate you in every way. Until our eyes meet again, may you be filled with love and blessed in every way.

Sid McNairy

Preface

There is a fire that propels you in the spirit of becoming a warrior. Sid McNairy's mission is that of the Nahi Warrior. His purpose in life, to evolve all beings to a way of peaceful existence, is something I can truly stand behind. I met Sid at a meditation ceremony in 2016, and every moment that we've connected since has led to bringing this book forward. Working on the book has been an eye-opening experience, challenging me in new directions and witnessing new reflections, as have many moments in our time knowing each other. I am honored to be a part of supporting you in this way and thank you, Sid, for the space we have shared and for your pursuit in elevating the masses and inspiring the hearts of many to live with purpose, ease, and grace. You have been a friend and a mentor to me, and I am grateful to have met you.

This book is a guide to follow in finding your own peace within and having faith in being able to champion your life in a way you may have never dreamt possible. There are two parts to this book. As you turn each page, you will take a walk through Sid's evolution. His lessons and examples of overcoming his own obstacles and his self-realization in life will help you to be able to land as a pillar of peace for all. His life and experiences as a college football coach, turned yogi and spiritual teacher, and through the Native American culture he was initiated into, as well as other various spiritual learning he has met along the way, provide the content of insight and teachings for this book.

In the first part, Sid speaks of the Four Cornerstones as a support system that can guide us in accessing something greater than what we think we know in order to win at the universal game of life. He reveals, first, what it is to play small when you play the game as a victim. Secondly, he touches on the difference between what is real and what is perspective, the labels we identify with, and the stories we create in our minds that affect and attract what it is we are asking for. Thirdly, he conveys how, if we hold onto resistance, we block ourselves from learning from our own inner wisdom and the opportunity to live in the flow of it all with great ease. Last, but not least, he challenges us to sit with things and relinquish the need to control or react, and instead to be present and aware to allow the mind to move into stillness by being okay with all that is.

Sid was compelled to write this book as he recognized the many who are oblivious to how they play and land in the spirit of the game we call life, and how many operate from only a fraction of their capacity for living a fulfilling life rooted in love, strength, and happiness. He became aware of this as early as the age of three, sitting in the pews of his church, that many were asleep to what was possible in their understanding of what it is to truly "be," to be awake and to be at peace. He knew then that he was meant to lead others. His mission in life was gradually revealed on a much deeper level as time would pass, and he is now able to live it, to give it. I have personally witnessed the shifts that have taken place in the lives of many who have crossed paths with Sid in the past couple of years, including my own.

In the second part of this book, you will get a glimpse into unlocking the great mystery of that which holds you back from discovering your own "Champion Warrior." You will start to awaken as you dismantle your preconceived notions or reasons for living and being less than your highest self. Sid uses the parallels of an elite athlete in sports, along with his lessons in coaching and our ways of being on the field of life, to relate the heart of a Champion Warrior and the places or pitfalls that may cause us to get stuck or stifled, and ultimately, enable our own suffering from living in a lower vibration. Sid helps us to understand how we can take ownership in how our reality is being shaped when we resist faith in staying open, due to the constraints of perceptions from our past experiences, and how this ultimately separates us from union, disconnecting us from God. He opens our eyes in seeing that a true Warrior on a quest of any kind is relentless in reaching for greatness. He or she is willing to learn through forgiveness, rebuilding, and commitment; to practice attracting a new future, via conscious choice in every moment; and to give way to accessing the heart, that space where only love resides, so that transformation can begin and lead to landing in a strong foundation of integrity.

May this book inspire you to watch and understand yourself. May you be willing to see the reflections within, in order to transform and truly know yourself. May you move beyond fear and doubt, and release the bonds of all negative emotion that may sabotage or hinder your growth towards navigating and operating in peace and love for all. May you be motivated to do the work in removing your conditions and step into acceptance in holding yourself accountable and finding gratitude in everything, so that you may cultivate the Warrior within and start manifesting and living your dreams. May this book encourage you to walk a path of love for all of your days and be the change the world so desperately needs. May your heart land and remain in peace. May you live it consciously, so that your family and loved ones, friends, colleagues, and strangers alike see you as the example within your communities, and eventually the world, as the ripple effect starts to take form, so that they, too, may be inspired to be the change they seek, and bring forward the life they desire. The Nahi Warrior knows there won't be peace until all have peace.

Namaste,
Elyssa Williams

A Warrior's Prayer

I call on the Four Directions, as you have set up the pillars in my life on the mountain.

To the keepers of the East, the Great Eagle, may you come in and give us and those reading this book the vision to continue to grow and heal in every way, so that all creatures on this planet and those who are not on this planet any more, can feel it through this book from your eyes, from your vision that connects us to our highest. As you fly the highest of all the beings here, may you lift this book up, as well.

To the keepers of the South, I ask that you come in and continue to bring in the reflection that we see in one another, the reflection of the coyote and the mouse, so people can understand how to let go of sweating the small things and begin to embrace all that is in your way.

To the keepers of the West, Brother Bear, I ask of you to send your medicine and your healing into this book as you have done in my life, allowing everyone to look within to find their space of healing that helps us all heal in every way.

To the keepers of the North, the Grandmothers, the White Buffalo, the White Buffalo Woman who carried the peace pipe, can you give us the wisdom so that this book will heal hearts and create a deep sense of peace throughout every being that reads the Warrior Within. And from this space of peace, let them feel the love that flows from you to all of us.

To all of our relations, to the winged ones, the birds that fly through the sky, to the creepy crawlers that move on the earth, to the trees, the spirits, and all the others that I may be missing: may you join us as you have joined me on the mountain. Please come into this book and share your wisdom.

To Mother earth, you have provided us everything in the physical and held us in your arms when we have fallen apart. May you come with us and allow this book to have deep roots so we can help others reconnect to you so they can see their reflection of hurt is causing the hurt on the earth and that when they heal them- selves, they will heal you.

And to Creator, the Great Mystery that lies within each of us, can we begin to know through this book who we really are in truth beyond the physical realm, beyond the money, beyond everything that holds us back in our fears so we can let go of the illusions and understand that through your love we have everything.

PART ONE

THE BIRTH OF A NAHI WARRIOR

CORNERSTONE ONE

How to Process the Game: Letting Go of Victim Consciousness

The four cornerstones are here to build the foundation of a solid spiritual practice and aid you in living awake as a Champion Warrior. The four cornerstones will allow you the space to operate, to produce the life and the moments you desire, and to bring forward peace in all ways. The four cornerstones consist of understanding the process of the universal game of life, understanding the effects of science on life, going with the flow, and living with a warrior's heart, grounded in peace. Having four cornerstones to land in will give you a solid support system needed to find peace and open to the power of faith. Through this support, the connections give way to landing into a state of People Everywhere Achieving Creative Ease (P.E.A.C.E). It is the Champion Warrior within that allows access to something greater than ourselves to help us grow.

The first cornerstone is to understand how to process the universal game of life in order to let go of victim consciousness. With this cornerstone you realize you are no longer a victim to life. It is the process of the game that allows us to sharpen our tools to perform at a higher level through the game. The practice requires creating drills to formulate what is needed in our lives. These drills become tools that give us an opportunity to study ourselves to see how we can perform better when we actually hit the field running in the universal game of life.

Our yoga practice is a great example or reflection of seeing how you perform in the game of life. When you are on your yoga mat, you actually get a chance to look and study where you are, to see *you*, what you do, how you shape things, how you land in your foundation, as you observe all the things that come forward for you. When we fidget, wipe the sweat, or come out of a posture early, as the posture gets tough, it is a reflection of our reactions to moments in our lives that get tough as well. In our yoga practice, the way we operate and the way we move from posture to posture resembles some aspect of how we move in our daily living.

Be willing to study yourself. This practice here on earth is just that, a *practice*, not a *perfect*. We are perfect inwardly. Our inward perfection, or our *in-perfections*, are actually looking at us on the inside to understand where we are perfect.

Our breath is another tool to utilize in seeing ourselves within the practice. When our breath becomes short and choppy, we are speaking and relaying to our body that there is a panic within. Telling ourselves that something is too hard then causes tension to build in our body. The opposite can be said when our breath is long and lengthened out, causing us to find a steadiness that speaks to our body. When that steadiness comes in, we will find that we actually gain more power through our breath, along with a deeper understanding of where we are and how we connect to the infinite source that gives us a greater sense of power and freedom within. It is in our observation and awareness of our breath that we are able to learn to witness our reaction to the moments in life.

Have you ever wished for your life to be changed? To bring in a new way? What is the game for you? You can and will change it. You will never desire to go back, even though you could if you chose to. Open up, and trust in the moment. There is a journey we are all on. If you have this book in hand, the journey you are on is the journey of a warrior. Today is the moment you have been waiting for, the moment when all things come to be. I am here for you in this moment, and I make one solid promise: I am going to be with you to help guide you on your quest for peace. The time is now, so let's go.

As I sit in a plane flying to Sedona, Arizona, I begin to reflect on the many moments of my life and where I am today. I have come to realize that so much has taken place on this journey to allow me to open up to the power that lies within. It is by looking inside that we all have the opportunity to remember just who we are and why we are here. I have come to discover that I am here to connect with others, to recognize the divinity within, and to grow in every way. My road has been different, yet very much the same. I came in with a mission—to bring peace to the world—and along the way I forgot. In this forgetting, I became lost as I further disconnected from the source of all love within.

Anger has reared its ugly head in many instances along the way. By sharing my journey with you, I know that you, and many before, will have an opportunity to reflect and find peace in your way. Life has been a series of moments and connections with old and new friends that has brought me here now. Through the igniting and rising energy within, which is shared and received, I am compelled and motivated to persevere on my quest for peace. As you dive into your spirit and this book, may you feel the energy within you ignite and build with every page. May you find that the lessons I have learned, as many do on the field of life, help you to move forward in a way that serves your highest good. The lessons I have received from the games have allowed me to walk the path and find the zone through all of life's moments. As you connect with those you meet, stay open and touch another's heart as well.

It is this game that continues to help me elevate in every way. I can recall the moment I sat down with an old friend and began to reflect on the struggle she was in. Sharon was sitting in her stuff, and everyone in her life seemed to have great advice about ways for her to change. The problem appeared to be that Sharon was caught in a web of repetitive patterns. I remember her stating that although she was in a different marriage, she felt as though she was in the same place where she had been in her previous marriage. She wanted advice. I recalled the many elders I listened to before, who rarely said what to do. They would tell stories that would help you find the answers that lie within yourself.

I began to explain, as we waited for our lunch, how people are like silverware. We have forks, spoons, and knives, all of which can work well together. You often need a fork and knife to cut your food. But for some reason when we put them away, we lay the spoons with the spoons, we stack the forks with the forks, and place the knives side by side. And, when it is time to clean them in the dishwasher, if they stay together, they never get clean. Here is the key: no matter if it is a fork, spoon, or knife, if you melt them down you can transform them to whatever you want. It is like that in our own relationships. If we strip down our beliefs, let go of what we do, and forget about the concepts of our way of being, we will find that we are the same.

Once we figure out that fact, we have a chance to connect again to the nothingness from where we came. From nothing, all things are born. This is commonly overlooked in sports, where coaches have a preconceived notion of the players. The same holds true in most relationships we encounter in our lives. If we can eliminate the notions, assumptions, and predetermined expectations, we can see we are the same.

Sharon and I would visit many more times over the years. We could see how the shifts were taking place within each of us, and it was amazing to witness how we both had healed so much inside and that we were able to find how love has truly landed in both our lives.

My journey has been that of a Nahi Warrior, and it is how I continue to maintain peace in every way. A major part of my journey has taken place on the Native American vision quest, and it is where I recalled my mission on earth. At the end of each vision quest we come back from sitting out and finish with a sweat-lodge ceremony. What was amazing on this particular vision quest was that my parents had come to support me. During the break between the third and fourth round of the ceremony, everyone had an opportunity to share. We went around and my father decided to speak. He started off by saying he was proud of me for going out and sitting over night. Both of my parents were scared at times for my life, knowing that all the animals were out and their son had nothing between himself and the animals. My dad went on to explain that growing up I was always tough. There were times that I would play in soccer games with a 103 degree temperature, endure full blown asthma attacks, or even play in a game with three broken toes on my kicking foot. He spoke of how, before I was born, he had gone through a tough time in his life, and he remembered praying for help. He asked God to send a prophet to help him see where he could shift his life. He concluded, "My son, whom you all call Sid, was sent to me that day."

I once got to see my dad give a speech at Morgan State University while I was coaching. He took a moment to introduce me. He started by saying, "I want you to meet my son; we thought about naming him Jesus and thought it was too much pressure, so we named him Sid."

Performing in the universal game of life is still just a practice. We have lived in these three dimensions of life for far too long. These three dimensions consist of the past, the present, and the future. Living in those three dimensions, we have continued to bring forward the tragedies that have happened around us. You can see this with teams. Teams that are losing continue to stay along the same path. It is by shifting our vision, in the way that God moved in creating the earth, that we truly become the creators that we are meant to be. Then we create a reality that opens up to winning in all ways, and winning with love. That creation originated with an energy that started the earth. The future was created by the first vibration, the same way our thoughts are created. Our thoughts are simply vibrations that create and carry forward. Once we move into the now, it is immediately gone. What came after creation of the earth, is the past. History has been written in books, and we continue to study and do the same things over and over.

It is by shifting ourselves into the four dimensions of creation that we will change our own reality. These four dimensions are going from creating future in the present moment. When we are in the present moment, we then step into the next moment, creating the past moment. These are the four dimensions: Future to present, now to past. Future to present, now to past. Future to present, now to past. It is in the creation of a vision of our lives that we are able to create what is coming next.

I can see this when I look back at Northwestern University in the 90's, with Gary Barnett. He set the tone, he recruited everyone into his system, and they went on to win. Those who were living in the three dimensions, versus Gary Barnett's new creation of four dimensions, continued to look at the past Northwestern losers being the present moment and continuing in that future. But what Gary Barnett did was recruit people to come to believe in his mission, his vision—just like you can do in your life. He recruited players, most of whom did not have the ability to go on to play in the NFL. But they were recruited to be part of a vision of becoming winners, so they had a future that became their present moment, and they went on to create the now, and a past history, of Northwestern's football team winning the Rose Bowl.

Where in your life can you now live a present moment, which shifts into being the past of your own future? Where you aren't getting stuck in the future thoughts of where you are going, but actually creating them right now in the steps and action that you are taking? When *where you are at*, eventually becomes *what has been*. Open up to seeing the four dimensions, beyond the three-dimensional world we've been stuck in for so long.

"I am no longer a victim; I have created my life."

On June 26, 1970, I arrived early in the morning. It seems to me that I was smiling, excited because I had chosen my parents for many lessons that would come forward as time would pass. Born to Mrs. Bobbie Lee McNairy and Dr. Sidney A. McNairy, Jr., two people who have made it out of the projects of Memphis, Tennessee, to begin a life that would pave the way for me to be where I am today. It was in Baton Rouge, Louisiana, where many of the stories in my head began. Some of these I remember clear as day, while others have grown stronger with time.

My early years were great. I remember being so happy, happy just seeing myself and my reflection. My mom had set mirrors around my baby crib. You know the ones, with the toys on the bottom that make noises, and you, the baby, feel like you are playing with another baby. It seems I learned to play and enjoy time alone from those early moments. I opened up to seeing myself and loving the reflection. It took some time to understand why I would pause in mirrors, for no reason at all, just to look into my own eyes.

I have felt this way since my earliest memories. The first time I recall it consciously was when I was about three and a half years old. The Immaculate Conception Catholic Church, our cathedral in Baton Rouge, Louisiana, was the place to be on Sunday, even above football. There was an altar with a huge cross with Christ on it. Father Enette would greet us at the door every week. He called me his boy, so it always felt loving to be there. I'd sit in the pew and look around. It seems to me that I was always in deep thought, even if I didn't have the words to share it. I remember one particular Sunday, shortly before my fourth birthday, I sat observing and studying everyone in the room. My father sat to my left at the edge of the aisle and my sister to my right. As I watched, I came to the conclusion that everyone was asleep. I remember thinking, *wake up!* I am here! I can help you! I looked to the front of the church and had my first inclination that I would stand and lead everyone. I knew my mission was anchored in my heart of hearts. I knew in that moment that I was there to deliver peace to the world. I looked around and my eyes landed again on my dad. I could see that he was a powerful man, a noble man who wanted peace.

My parents had always instilled in me the idea that, as an African American man, I had to do everything better than anyone else. They told me that there was nothing that I couldn't do. So it seemed logical to me as a child, that if Jesus, a white Caucasian man, could walk on water—then I must be able to do that, too.

For a long time I wanted to actually walk on water, but now it has become a metaphor for a way of life: if I can connect with enough stillness, if I can cultivate a deep peace within that can never be rattled, then I can walk on water. The moment that I lose that peace, then I sink.

One of my biggest teachings is about reflections. We are all reflecting off one another all the time. We, as human beings, are 80 percent water, so imagine that when we meet each other, it is like meeting a lake of reflection. Each person is a reflection of our own inner selves. So when we are confronted by someone who takes us out of our own peace, we need to look within, and see where that peace is missing inside of us. When you look at another person, can you walk on that water that you are seeing in the other person? Can you keep the peace inside that keeps the peace for all of us? Can you hold that reflection of peace inside of you?

I would later come to understand the plight of a man of color, and that this plight would cause a disruption to peace in one's soul. I'd come to find in those moments a purpose that would initiate taking on the anger of my father, my father's father, and all the seven generations before me.

In our lives we have moments that shape us and bring forward a cycle that may need to be shifted, if we are to live in peace. I had a perspective of believing I was right and everyone else was wrong. I would go on to feel a need to defend what was right, through my eyes, for many years to come. Later in life, I had to break that habit of winning at all cost, even though there was, and still is, a burning desire inside to reach for my best!

After my fourth birthday, I had a moment when I would try on this new stance. Again, it seemed to coincide with Sunday church. I was a skinny boy, who really only wanted to eat when I felt I had to. So one Sunday, as we got ready for church, I decided not to eat. My dad had eaten everything on his plate and was going to finish getting dressed. He said, "Son, when I am dressed we will be leaving for church, and those eggs you have better be finished." There I sat, looking at those eggs, knowing I did not want to eat. So I made a conscious choice to put my eggs in my mouth, to not chew them, and to never swallow them. When my dad came out he said, "Good job, now let's go."

We headed to church, and all I could think about were those eggs. After mass, as we usually did, we paused outside to say hi to Father Ennette. This day he went to tickle me, and I pulled away, grabbing my dad's leg.

"What's wrong with Sid?" he asked, looking at my dad. They were great friends. He looked at me and asked again, "Sid, what is wrong with my boy?"

I began to cry. My dad took me off to the side and Father Ennette leaned in when my dad asked what was wrong. He could tell I had something in my mouth. As he got me to open my mouth, Father Ennette almost threw up at the sight and smell of the two-hours-old eggs, liquified in my mouth. I was stubborn and knew I was right. I should eat when I wanted, and no one should tell me when that is. To this day, I eat at a different rhythm than most.

When we got home that day, I became silent and angry. I did not want to speak, and I remember I would be playing with my legos, and my dad would come and want to play with me. I would turn my back and play alone. This would continue for the next four months, and in time, I would come to make a choice: of wanting to be right or of wanting to be happy. My mom would later tell me how heartbroken this made my dad feel. I am sure as time passed, this put an unneeded strain on our relationship.

I had a big temper early on and was really stubborn about what I perceived as right. I recall going into the woods with my friend Carlton. He was an older kid who would take care of me around the neighborhood. Growing up in Baton Rouge, we spent a lot of time outside, hiking deep into the woods. Carlton used to give me piggyback rides when I couldn't keep up. There was one day when I climbed off his back and saw this amazing small pine tree made out of sand. I wasn't sure what it was, but I was curious to find out. I stepped back and kicked with all my might. To my amazement, it was full of fire ants that swarmed me relentlessly. I began dancing; you know, the old ants-in-your-pants dance. They were not happy I had invaded their domain and were merciless in their pursuit of letting me know, biting me all over. Carlton put me on his back again and ran straight to the house. Fortunately for me, my mom knew exactly what to do. She ran a bath and dumped me in. Once I was in the tub, she took off my clothes, and the ants began to drown. Then she took me out of the bath and helped clear the bites. I cried a bit, and yet I wanted to go back.

I was only five years old, and in some ways not the smartest. A couple of days would pass, and we would go back, deep into the woods, where I thought I could get revenge. Little did I know, it seemed like the ants knew I was coming. Carlton put me down again, and I gave it another go. With such determination and with all my force, I kicked yet another mound. Even as I began to run home, they still seemed to be covering my body. My mom tended to me once again, through the same ordeal. It was a quick lesson in learning how to be with, and respect nature. Those ants were a fierce community and stuck together no matter what. I began to understand that I would learn to stick with my community in the same way. I also learned that revenge really only comes back to bite you in the butt. No pun intended. So never burn your bridges.

When I was about six years old, we moved from Baton Rouge to Washington, DC. It seemed like a good place to go. In the transition of the move, we stayed in a hotel where my dad would teach me how to play chess. I liked the game because I could move all the pieces the way I wanted. It taught me a lot in the ways of how to think strategically in anticipating what my opponent would do next, and how to concentrate and take my time in moving—all valuable tools that would serve me later in life in my coaching and teaching.

I related to this game from the very beginning, as if we human beings were the pieces on the chess set, and that something was moving us around in this life. I knew I wanted to be a king. It seemed as though everyone cared about the king and that the king was very important. I knew I wanted to find a queen because she was so powerful, she could do it all on the board. Yet I wanted to know who is actually controlling me? Who was watching me as I moved around this world? This question would go on to challenge my mind for the rest of my life. I still today, love that game of chess.

So many things are clear for me. I have been blessed to see the many defining moments of my life, which have continued to allow me to see the lessons that have led me to a deeper understanding of how we can all live. We had just moved to the DC/Maryland/Virginia area, and our family had finally settled into our new home. My dad was able to get his new car, a silver 260Z. He was really happy with his new car. He even drove my mom's car to work so he could figure out where to park it, in order to protect the car.

I asked my mom if I could go outside to play. It was what I was used to, having grown up in Baton Rouge. When I got outside, there was a kid who found humor in making fun of my southern accent. He would tease me, and then run around the car. He was a little older. Since I couldn't catch him, as I passed by I noticed a big rock. I thought if I throw this rock at him, I can hurt him, and then he'll stop making fun of me. Boy, was that a bad call. I picked up the rock and launched it at him. It landed right in the middle of my dad's new car. I went into the house and looked at my mom. She looked up at me, and I knew that look. "What did you do, Sidney," she asked.

I said, "Well, I threw a rock at the boy down the street."

She came out and saw the boulder in the middle of my dad's car. She said, "Boy, get in the house. I am not sure what we should do. Go and sit on the stool until your dad gets home."

Now this was 3:00 p.m., and my dad never got home before 6:30, so I sat there for three hours. I remember feeling my chest tighten up. The more boxes my mom unpacked, the more the dust built in the air. I recall by the time my dad got home, I was so stressed, I couldn't breathe. What was funny is, as mad as my dad was about his car, he cared so much about me that he let go of that quickly. He helped me calm down and would spend the next eleven years helping me learn how to release and control my temper. It seems crazy to me, how I would spend the next twenty-seven years learning from my asthma and allergies that had developed that day.

We all have something that takes place during our childhood that will cause us to realize we are not enough of something in the moment, so we adapt to something new just to protect ourselves. Over many years to come, my asthma would show up when I was stressed, and I had no way of handling it. Everything that has transpired in my life has helped me to evolve in a new light.

From that moment forward, it seemed that my parents would help me find ways to harness my energy. I was set to play for my dad's recreational soccer team. It was great learning, being put in a position to be aggressive. I was playing goalie, so I was willing to attack the ball. We were a few games in when a bigger team saw what I and a couple of my teammates could do. We were recruited and asked to show up at tryouts for a select team, in Montgomery Village. Tryouts were pretty easy. In our minds, we just did what we do. For some reason, the coaches saw that I would be great out in the field, as opposed to playing in the goal. We made the team, and my soccer career would continue to grow from there. What was great was that, at eight years old, I was taught to train my mind, to meditate, and to go into myself to learn how to bring forward what I desired.

Family was really big for us. We had a huge family. My Grandmother Mary, on my dad's side, had twenty-one siblings, so when we would have a full family reunion, we could have as many as one hundred fifty people there. We had a great re-union in Detroit one year. Everyone laughing and partying. A small group of us one night went over to Canada to have din-ner. Detroit to Toronto was a quick trip. We visited the Niagara Falls. It was an experience of every emotion; I was amazed, happy, and then scared. The power of the falls felt like I could be swept off at any point. We had a blast getting soaking wet and seeing things I had never seen before. We ended up at a casino that had go-carts and an arcade to occupy the kids, while the parents went and did their thing.

After the daytime fun, we all changed and went to dinner. This was the first time I remember seeing someone drink al-cohol and begin to be ignorant. This moment began a deeper understanding that alcohol was not really something I wanted in my life. My Aunt Lucille was very dark-complected. All of a sudden, a man who was stumbling came over and started call-ing my aunt an ape. My uncle and dad asked the man to please allow us to have dinner in peace. For the next hour, this guy continued to yell obscenities. It was a lot to watch. We finished, paid for dinner, and were leaving when the guy decided to follow us out and continue to run his mouth. My dad was close to going after the guy, until the man's wife came and took him away. My Uncle Alvin, my aunt's husband, was a peaceful man. He comforted his wife, calmed my dad down, and we left without a major fight breaking out.

I remember my dad taking the time to make sure I learned from any situation, much like I would parent my kids later. He told me that it was not okay for anyone to be mean to another. He said that we should always stand up for people who are being mistreated. He also told me that I should not ever start a fight, and yet it was okay to finish any fight. The only time it was okay to start a fight was if I was called a nigger, or if someone was a threat to my mom. From that day forward, I knew I had a right to crush anyone, especially for the two situations he had told me of. I had a temper, and I was quick with my fist, so I felt I was ready to defend myself or anyone else in need.

Looking back, this was one of the many incidents that solidified me giving my power to the outside world. It would take many years for me to recognize what Mahatma Gandhi and Dr. Martin Luther King Jr. were helping to bring forward in the lives of many. By accessing peace and learning to *be* peace, we can all bring forward a shift beyond that of the control of others outside of ourselves.

As time would pass and I grew older, we would play in tournaments all over the place. We would play teams from other countries. One night I was playing with my cousin and my brother David. I had gotten angry and ran to get my cousin. When I chased after him, I hit my foot on the corner of the wall. I broke three toes on my right foot. This was my dominant kicking foot. The next day, my dad taped my foot, and Coach Stephens said I could play if I felt I could. It was the first game that I scored three goals. I played great. We made it to the finals. We were going to face the Wolverines from Canada. They had this kid who was awesome. He scored at will. He was five feet ten and much heavier than every kid around. Our coach decided that it would be best if I marked him the entire game. I was just supposed to mark him, never let him touch the ball, and make sure he did not score. At the start of the game, I was on it in the first ten minutes. He never got to touch the ball. No matter where he went on the field, I followed him. He began to get frustrated, at one point saying, "Get away from me, you little nigger!"

Remember, I was told fighting was not an option, with the two exceptions of course, and this kid had just delivered one of them. From that moment on, I crushed him. I would cut him down every chance I could. There were a couple of times that we ended up in a pushing match, and both of us received warnings. If we continued, we would be thrown out of the game. We ended up winning the game, and the championship.

After the game, the opposing player came up and said, "Hey, sorry—you are the toughest guy I have ever played against. Nice game."

On the way home my dad shared his excitement of how great he thought I'd played. "You scored, and you guarded that big kid," he said with pride. He asked me how I did it.

I smiled and said, "He called me a nigger."

Funny how life can help some fold, and others respond. It was the warrior in me that continued to grow, in every moment that came up. Meditation would continue to move in and out of my life, and continues to remain today. One of the triggers that would bring on my asthma was the stress of living up to the expectations of others. During the early years of my soccer career, I would often spend Friday nights with a temperature of 103, yet play games on Saturdays. It was during these moments that I would be able to fine-tune my focus and play at the top of my game. It didn't matter what affliction would test me, I would be able to channel any pain into performing at my best.

As the years would pass, I would embrace sports as a way of seeing my reflection. Playing every sport possible as a kid helped to shape my existence today. Learning to play through anything has given me the ability to work, when most would quit. I recall being sick several times. Once with a fever of 103 degrees, I had one of my best games, scoring more and playing with a focus like no other. Because of moments like these, I came away knowing my spirit could shine through and give me access to the strength from deep within.

When I went to play soccer in England, I faced an even greater challenge. I went blind for a couple of days. The pollen count was so high that I woke up with sleep caps on my eyes. When the caps came off, I was unable to see. This was a huge test, to be fifteen, losing my sight, in a foreign country, away from my family. I can remember going to see the doctor and feeling like there was nothing to do but ask for help, to look to something bigger than myself, to help me see again. After running a few tests, the doctor told me and the host mom I was staying with that I would more than likely get my sight back, but only time would tell. We returned back home. I remember I was left feeling okay, that all I really wanted was to get my sight back so that I could practice in two days. We were given the day off, and I was to rest and wait and see.

Later, we called back to the states. It seemed to be a challenge for my mom to get on the phone. As my host mom talked to her, they both began crying. My dad asked to speak to me. When we spoke, I felt his concern, but I believed that, even at fifteen, I knew where I was. I recall this being learned over time. Any time I was injured, my dad would yell from the sidelines, "get up!" I would, and rather quickly. This was tough for some of the other parents to hear. Some parents would actually cringe and get upset that my dad would just yell for me to get up. I later learned that this was empowerment and love, which lifted my spirit up beyond my mind. So in this moment, when my dad checked in to see how I was, I knew and told him that, from the faith in me, I knew I was okay. And in that same moment, he knew that I was going to be just fine. They never flew to see me in England because I said I could handle it. In the end, I went back to practice a day later, played with partial sight, and again, learned my strength from within was there and available to be accessed at any given moment. I learned to have faith in me, and in something bigger. It would take even longer for me to let others in to help me in the future.

After going to play in England, I really wanted to leave school and just go and play soccer overseas. This seemed like a great opportunity. I had played well and was told I could play in the farm leagues. My parents said, "Not a chance." My dad was a very intellectual man. Even to this day, I feel I have yet to meet someone whose brain operates at a faster rate. You could take a calculator, call out any number, multiply or divide it by any other number, and before you could hit enter, he would tell you the answer. Heck, I hated playing scrabble with my parents, because my dad had memorized every word in the dictionary by third grade. My mom was brilliant as well, writing textbooks in her summers for the Montgomery County School District. So staying to play sport and dropping out of school was not an option. Here marks when I decided it was time to play football.

My first year in football, I had no clue what it was like to wear pads. I mean playing street ball, no one could ever tackle me. Now in a real game and in pads, it was different, and I decided not to play. I kept playing soccer and continued to study the game and figure out how to play. I also ran track. The varsity, head football coach asked who the tenth grader was that ran so fast. We won the state championship in track all three years I was in high school. It was a great experience to get into a sport that truly matched your talents. I loved looking up to the older athletes and being inspired to be a leader as I got older.

John Harvill was the head coach of our high-school football team. He was an amazing human being. He touched so many lives. I recall him being the reason I wanted to coach when I got older. The family connection he created was awesome. I wanted to touch lives as he had mine. Many years after high school, he would still look after me because I was one of his guys. He had done so much with his life, all of which was an inspiration for me. He had gone to war, played baseball in college, and was a tremendous football coach.

My junior year he had recruited so many people to come and play football. The coaches were all great guys. Coach Joyce, my junior-high gym teacher, was our defensive coordinator and coached our field events for track. Coach Perry coached our receivers and defensive backs. He was also our track coach. Coach Kephart was also a coach, who later became the head coach at our high school. What is amazing is how these coaches coached all year round, in between football and indoor and outdoor track. They truly helped shape my life and who I am today.

Many years after high school, when I became a college coach, Coach Harvill and Coach Joyce would grab me at the National Coaches Convention and have breakfast with me or go and watch a clinic. I am forever grateful for the impact these great men had on my life.

Outside all the amazing moments I could talk about with our football teams, the great games, and the comeback win in the state championship game, what I recall most is that before every game our coaches would leave us in the gym, turn off the lights, and have us sit quietly and focus on the task at hand. We would always turn up and come out ready to play. Meditation continued as a fundamental practice for me, no matter who my coaches were, no matter what sport. Some remember the games, and I remember those, yet what has stayed with me from eight years old is all the coaches that continued to help me meditate and focus myself to be the best.

Our junior year was amazing, with a stacked team. The seniors were such great players that it was hard to get as much playing time on the field. It was also exciting because we went all the way and won the state championship. Life was fun, and football was life for me in many ways. Even though I never voiced to my parents why I really chose to play football, they supported me anyway. From then on, I would go back and forth between football and soccer.

My senior year of football was fun, yet we had lost so many great players. Although we had several people who went on to play college ball, we just weren't the same. Track, on the other hand that year, was great. I went on to being the captain of the team and kept our streak going.

In college, I continued to find the desire to be me and to lead in many ways. I attended Purdue University in Indiana, with the intention of being an engineer. I walked onto campus as a football player. Little did I know, my calling would take me back to playing soccer. I was used to being with athletes. My whole life had been about sports and meditation, so this is what I figured would be the same in college.

In my freshman year, I became friends with a lot of people. It was an environment that seemed to fit within the comfort zone of my past. Minorities, though, were only 2 percent of the student body. So to survive, you became friends with everyone, no matter race or gender. I recall my friends from the dorm coming and asking me to go see fraternities with them. Now, mind you, my dad was an Alpha and my uncle was a Kappa, both of which, historically, were African American fraternities. I did not learn much about their experiences, so I was pretty open to whatever would come. We visited several fraternities, one of which caught my eye, really because the members were mostly athletes. I continued on, following my friends towards Delta Tau Delta. I was approached, and asked to join.

I was told they thought I was the guy that could help integrate the fraternity system. Now, mind you, Purdue was the second-largest Greek system in the country, and there had never been mixing of races. Near by in Crown Point, Indiana, they were still burning crosses in the front yards of houses where blacks lived. So for me this was an opportunity to do something that would shape people for many years to come. There were times in dealing with other fraternities, and times on campus, where I was called a nigger. It never ended well for the other guy, and it left a mark in me that would take years to heal.

We started with twenty-six guys in our pledge class. Hell night was the last night of the initiation process at Delta Tau Delta, the Gamma Lambda chapter, where alumni could come back and haze the pledges. By this time, I had already become really close with my pledge brothers and tight with everyone in the fraternity. This night was bigger than any other, it seemed like three hundred guys had come back to make sure the black guy did not make it through. They took our pledge class up to the attic to keep us away from the alumni. We sat in the room and began to talk about how we would all go out fighting. Several of us competed in fraternity boxing matches on campus, called Boiler Bouts. Darren and Ben were heavyweights, Marko was our middleweight, and I was our lightweight. So when it came time, we were all ready to go to war for each other, anticipating an all-out brawl. Apparently, this was realized by the rest of the fraternity, and this portion of the pledging process had been cancelled at the last minute. We finished the night with a huge party, one of many to come.

There was one guy in the fraternity who really did not want me to pledge. In the midst of hell night, he brought me into his room. I was nervous, which meant I was ready to fight. I walked in, he got out two beers, and said he wanted to talk. He said he was intrigued and amazed at the person I was, and he wanted to know me and why I was doing what I was. I probably had one of the easiest hell nights in the history of the fraternity. Later, he would become a guy I looked up to. We can break barriers in so many ways, by just moving beyond our fears. I am glad I had this experience, even though I have not done much since college in the name of Greek life.

My twenty-first birthday was a bit more eventful compared to what most people seemed to experience. My dear friend Ben had this great Mercedes that we drove everywhere. We headed to Dayton, Ohio, in it the day before I turned twenty-one, as soon as he got word that his uncle had been in a boating accident and had taken an anchor to the skull. He was lucky because the boat he hit was owned by a doctor, who was able to immediately tend to him, grabbing a bag of ice and covering his brain. He was never the same. Yet, his life was saved.

I turned twenty-one at midnight, and the drinking fest began as we celebrated. It was such a blur, I can barely remember everywhere we partied. I do remember we celebrated for a week straight. On the last night, we ended up getting the Buster Douglas vs. Mike Tyson fight on Pay Per View. We tapped a keg of beer and got a fifth of tequila. Tequila was not the best drink for me, usually resulting in me getting in a fight. Mike Tyson had lost one of the worse fights I had ever seen. Mind you, I loved watching Iron Mike fight. He was invincible in the ring. After he lost this fight, I was content with drinking the rest of the night away. It was my twenty-first birthday, and the examples I had of drinking were that you drank a lot. I drank so much I ended up blacking out at the end of the night.

On the way home, I was asked to stop in at a party that was above my apartment. The party consisted of four girls, my pledge mom, Lisa, and three of her sorority sisters. Yes, it was a fun summer. I went to the party, then went home and blacked out. I slept like a rock.

Come morning, I woke up to a woman screaming in my room. "Get out," she said. I was a little stunned, because I had no clue where I was. I looked around, realizing I was in my room.

"Wait a minute," I said. "You get out, this is my room."

"No, it isn't!"

"Um, yes, it is. Would you have pictures of models and sports on your walls?"

"Oh my gosh, how did I get here?"

"I don't know and really don't care—you have to go."

"I can't leave, I'm naked."

"Well, somehow you got here naked. I think you need to leave."

"Can I have some clothes?"

"No!"

"Please, my boyfriend is upstairs."

I ended up letting her wear my comforter out. Her boyfriend brought the comforter back. He went onto explain that she had a problem sleepwalking at night. He thought since my room was the same room set up as hers, she must have thought she was in her room when she got in bed. All I could think to myself was, if that works for you, I am home free. We parted ways, and I began to pay a little more attention to my life.

At this point in my life everything was happening to me. I was the victim of what may seem like a fraternity boy's fictional life. It all was beginning to set in. Lessons were being learned that alcohol was a common denominator and eventually I would learn to take control of my life.

Having almost been kicked out of school, having one too many chances of getting in serious trouble, it was time for me to buckle in, get serious about life, and get a degree.

My first three years of college were interesting. I was getting by in school, yet I couldn't find what it was that fueled my soul and allowed me to move forward with my life in a way that would be fulfilling. I had changed majors, played soccer, and still was searching for something more than drinking and partying.

I'm not even sure how the change happened. I went and registered for a few classes, sports history and sports psychology being two of them. There it was, a spark that would launch me into my future. I had fun learning for the first time ever in my life. I could not get enough. Heck, it made so much sense, I barely had to study. I would go on to get a degree in Movement and Sports Science. I would begin to experience life in a whole new way.

In my classes, I began to connect with the players of our football team. Again, it seemed I was about to experience yet another shift. I went on to become a personal trainer and started volunteering as a strength coach under Coach Big. This was where I would meet my best friend, Rick Smith, and get to know the twins, John and Joe O'Leary. We would have some great talks and begin to map out how life would unfold.

One night, John, Joe, and I were out studying. We began to talk about what was taking place around us. I recall John and Joe explaining different theories they had. They were twins, so they had been completing each other's thoughts long before I came around. There was this theory that John had, that we humans are nothing more than cells, and it was up to us to see how cells operated and then begin to operate at our highest. If earth is just a giant cell, then we have a nucleus, those who operate the main frame. We have those parts that are there to evaluate, to rid the main cell of the bad, in order to continue to move us forward. If we watch cells enough, we will learn more about ourselves. I would later come to understand how we all came from the first cell. It took what would help it grow, and it discarded all the rest. Once it had all of its greatness around, it divided itself in half and gave away what was best of itself to another. We, too, can live this way as well.

Another night we had a conversation around the Ten Commandments. I began to state how we have these guidelines that are actually leading us along the path of what we actually are looking to prevent. A baby doesn't come into the world knowing about what we are looking to prevent, so if we shift it, we can guide them to a direction of betterment for all.

Here is what I came up with:

1. Believe in the greatest of all.
2. Honor what is real.
3. Speak of the Lord with love.
4. Remember to take a day off and keep it holy.
5. Respect and give homage to those before you.
6. Help others live well.
7. Stay devoted to those you love.
8. Use what is yours, and share with those less fortunate.
9. Speak only what is real.
10. Be okay with what is yours.

We had many great moments. My first spring break was at South Padre Island. It was truly a drunken occasion, in true spring-break fashion. As I got older, I began to see more clearly that in the midst of every moment, a chance of something sacred existed. I remember when we went to Key West, we were out by the pool when a guy showed up and decided to share some wisdom. He seemed wise in my eyes, the spirit of his wife seemed to keep him younger, and he was happy. I had seen plenty of people who weren't happy, and whatever makes you happy seemed to be the way to go. He would go on to share something that would impact my life forever. He spoke of how we are all writing two books in life. Whichever has more in it will determine whether you feel content or not in your life. The first book we'll write will include the things you did not complete. The second will include the things you have. This has stayed with me ever since. What I learned from this was to make sure that the choices I make in life are something I am ready to live with. This random moment by the pool had truly shaped my life in a grand way.

I went on to help Rick Smith continue to build summer conditioning for the Purdue football team. Rick would become my best friend for many years to come. Rick and I would go on to experience life in so many great ways. I am blessed to have had him stand by me as my best man in my first marriage, become my eldest son's godfather, and walk side by side, together through so many moments in life. As time would pass, I would later discover why.

CORNERSTONE TWO
The Effects of Science on the Game

The second cornerstone takes us into a look at what are facts and perspectives, and how this shows up in the universal game of life. As we start to understand what is real and what we create in our mind, we begin to see how we can create all that is around us. In science we know that there are facts, things that are real, things that you have right in front of you. It is those facts that we build our life around. When something comes up, there is a moment—a real, life moment that takes place—and then we create a story around it, a vibration that comes from the fact, the actual thing taking place. That vibration leads us forward into creating a thought, a story around what is fact. The vibration continues and opens up to building a reality once again, which becomes another fact. So when we have a sensation in the body, often we label that sensation with a feeling, and that feeling is a story: sad, hurt, guilty, loving, joyful are all stories that have been built in the mind. Those stories ultimately attract the next thing in our reality. So when we look at science, we're sitting and beginning to discover how science is playing and impacting the game of life. As all become aware of the facts, open to the truth, and they manifest in their lives, everyone will move beyond fear.

It is in the facts and perspectives that we can truly attune ourselves to what is real or made up in our heads. Facts are a true moment that comes up in life. I like using the example of a coach and a player. The coach calls a meeting with one of his players. Fact, there is a meeting that is set up for the player. The player chooses it as good or bad. That is the beginning of a story in the player/coach relationship. Another fact comes up, being the first words that come out of the coach's mouth. All they are, are words in the meeting, fact. Then the player decides if those words are good or bad, story. This is where the player has actually decided to start creating a picture of what is actually real. Even though, in reality, the words coming out of the coach's mouth are just words. The player can then say, "This is great, coach just gave me the recipe to success"; or the same player could say, "Coach has just told me that I am going to be cut because I can't perform the way I thought I was performing." We all do this in life; we see from our perspective around the facts.

A baby is born, and we decide whether the baby will be great or not. Those are perspectives. A relationship breaks up, and we decide whether it was a catastrophe or a recipe for successful relationships later. It's important to see that in the game of life, we have the ability to create our perspective and the stories we wish to see. Take a moment, look at your own life, and see where you are creating a reality that is a disaster in your own perception. If you know that you want to have love in your life, but you are constantly creating stories around hate and anger, or guilt and shame, you get to be right. So if you begin to understand that, from there you can ask yourself: *how can I create the life I wish to have?*

Let's take a look at how science continues to play out in the game of life.

Isaac Newton gave us the three laws of motion.

Law number one: Every object in a state of uniform motion tends to remain in that state of motion, unless an external force is applied to it.

Law number two: The relationship between an object's mass, M, its acceleration, A, and the applied force, F, is stated as

$F = \mathbf{M} \times \mathbf{A}$. In this law, the direction of force vector is the same as the direction of the acceleration vector.

Law number three: For every action, there is an equal and opposite reaction.

Let's take a deeper look at the first law. Unless we decide to initiate an external force to what is taking place, we will continue to remain in the same motion we have been in. We are living in cycles, cycles that are ultimately continuing to move us along in the same path we have been on. Often this is hard for us to recognize because we have benefitted from living in this space. This is where Jesus's words, "Those who are last, will come first" can apply.

When we are in the midst of a spiritual bankruptcy, or life seems to be falling apart, it is easier for us to recognize what we want to change. When we have success as we know it—the big house, the car, the wife, the husband, the family, the kids—we often miss that we are having and living with less power than we are capable of. This is where we are living from our offensive and defensive playbook, which will be discussed later in detail. It is in this space, once we recognize it, that we are able to create a new space for ourselves. It is often easier for someone who is struggling to realize there is something better than where they are. So know that in your own life, wherever you are, there is an opportunity to shift, to dig in deeper, and to understand yourself at a deeper level all of the time. That self-study, the looking at yourself, is where you can be empowered to be whatever it is that you desire. Breaking down our old patterns is essential in order to shift, as is evolving past the need to respond and react to an outside force, to looking into yourself to align and shift where you are and choose to go next in life.

Newton's second law explains how force equals mass, times acceleration. The relationship between an object's mass and its acceleration equals its force. This applies to how quickly we are able to shift from one place to another. In my practice, I can see that when we have less mass, it will take less acceleration to get us to feel the outside force of where we are going. It is easily noted in the game of life, where we may need less outside force to understand our concept, or to integrate a shift in our lives.

When we have built fewer walls around what is impacting us, we are able to make a shift that creates an easier force to be understood and integrated, in order to shift our reality.

The third law describes how, for every action, there is an equal and opposite reaction. We live in a world of duality of action and reaction, and in order to have one, it is imperative that we accept and understand the other. There are two sides to every coin. On one side we may have hurt; on the other side, joy. On one side we may have happiness; on the other side, pain. On one side we may have love; on the other side, fear. When we decide to embrace one, we are able to open and embrace the other. When we resist, what we resist will persist.

In my life, this showed up in pushing away anger. It would be stuffed down, only to come up and explode later. Once I accepted that there was anger, I was able to embrace peace. I have lived with pains from many phases of life, from my childhood, from moving through high school and college, the pains of coaching, pains of parenting, and more. I recognized how all of this pain was landing in my body. By choosing to see and face them, and be with them, I started understanding that my desire for freedom was a hidden moment of wanting control, control that stemmed from my fears from many moments in my life.

One day, as I sat talking to another warrior, I began to explain that they had two bags of arrows lying by the fence of their life. As they moved forward in their life, there would come times when they would have to choose which bag of arrows they would use to tame their life. We are always choosing which arrows to use, our thoughts being the arrows that we launch. To operate in the second cornerstone, we must become more aware of how we are manifesting our reality from our thoughts. It is time for us to wake up and choose which arrows we will use. Arrows can often be hidden, and we may not see them clearly because wars are fought differently today. Wars are fought in the realm of many choosing to not see, and therefore they use their arrows unconsciously. Ignorance is actually quite the opposite of bliss. When we consciously choose our thoughts to lead us in the direction we want to go in life, we are choosing to use the arrows that direct us in a clear and steady direction.

When we consciously or unconsciously choose to use our thoughts to move in the direction of harm to ourselves, our loved ones, friends, or complete strangers, we are guiding our lives in a direction of destruction. Ultimately, we have chosen a poisonous arrow that will kill the fabric of the life we are aiming to lead. Poisonous arrows show up in several ways, in ways we often don't expect. They come forward during times of gossip, when we think we are talking about a person, telling a story about what we have perceived as a true timeline of life. They come forward in the moments when we think about a person and continue to hold on to what we don't like, because of our frustrations with the current events.

Poisonous arrows can also come forward from ourselves when we are being humble and reject a compliment, or have negative thoughts that put us down. I don't look good in this outfit. I am having a fat day. I can't write a book. On and on and on, we can destroy the love before it ever starts to build within ourselves. Being aware of self-talk is vital in creating the direction you desire to go. Using daily affirmations or mantras are tools that are always helpful in staying the course of where your thoughts can or will land.

Every day, every moment, I am picking up an arrow and taking aim.

The arrow I choose will continue to move me forward in the direction I want to go.

"I am the director of my life."

No matter how fast I am moving through life, I must be aware of every moment that comes my way and take aim for how I choose to move forward.

As I see where I am heading, I pause and take aim. It is in this moment that I realize I am the warrior.

As I begin to propel forward, I must take a moment, pause and pull back, so the universe can launch me forward into the next beautiful moment to come. I am willing to use the bow and arrow of my life, take aim, and go for it, in the direction I choose.

As I would enter into my coaching career I began to make a transition from living in the victim role and started to see how

I could manifest my life with conscious thought. I got my first coaching job in 1995, working with Bob Spoo, at Eastern Illinois University. Coach Spoo is one amazing human being. He helped me begin to move my fears of older white men, and I will forever be grateful for that. He truly was a father to me, in guiding me in becoming a great football coach. There were other great coaches I'd come to work for. Eric Holms at Northern Michigan University and Joe Novak at Northern Illinois University both would help me become a better person and coach in so many ways. Yet there is nothing like the love that I witnessed from Coach Spoo—something I continue to strive to be in the life of others to this day.

This same year, I made a decision to get married. Kind of an interesting choice, as my full name is Sidney Archie McNairy III, and I asked Cindy E. Archbold to marry me. It was always interesting when people would call the house and ask to speak to one of us. We often would have to ask for clarification about who exactly it was they wanted to speak with.

Then, just to keep it all interesting, March 30, 1995, my first son, Sid IV would be born. I was still coaching at EIU, and I was making $6,000 a year. I was working on my master's degree, and looking to continue a career that many thought was a waste of my Purdue education. I was offered a job working for the secret service after completing college. To give that up and choose to coach instead, was an interesting choice.

At the end of the season, Coach Spoo called me into his office and said, "I have a job for you." Mind you, I wanted to go and coach at Northern Illinois University. Coach told me he could get me to Northern Illinois University in a year and that I should consider going to Northern Michigan University to coach first. He asked, "Do you know where the Upper Peninsula is?" I sure as heck did not, only that it was above Michigan. Coach Holms called, and next thing I knew, I was on a flight for an interview. This was an interesting trip. My first flight was to Chicago O'Hare. It seemed like your everyday football trip. Then came the next two legs of this travel, a puddle hopper to Milwaukee, WI, then an even smaller plane to Marquette, MI. Every stop seemed like the great white north, as we boys from south of the

Mason-Dixon line would say. I arrived to find spring practice had already begun. Spring practice typically started in April, which was still two months away. There was still over one hundred inches of snow on the ground, and it was as cold as I had ever faced.

I met some great coaches while I was there. When I got back, I went in to talk to Coach Randy Melvin to discuss the possibility of taking this job. I shared how I wasn't sure if I wanted to go. The cold was a definite concern. I also wasn't really sure I wanted to leave the players and the coaches. He responded, "Man, they have a dome—and no matter where you go, there will be players you will bond with. What is important right now is you have a son on the way, and $6,000 a year will not cut it. You need benefits and money. I think you should take the job."

I would call Coach Holms and explain my situation. I explained that I was 15 credits short of my master's degree, and that I planned to sneak in a couple of classes so I could finish. I was already on a fast track, set to complete my degree in two years instead of three. I informed him that I also had a son on the way. He was great; he told me he could fly me back and forth. We would have practices Thursday evening through Monday morning. I would squeeze classes in and fly back as soon as I got word that Sid IV was coming.

Coaching at NMU was a lot of fun. We had a team that had gone 3-7, yet the players were hungry. We knew that with Coach Holms's offensive mind and Coach Kirby Cannon's defensive mind, we would be ready to win. It was a lot of work traveling back and forth, yet it was worth it. I would finish my degree, coach football, and make another step in my career. I felt all was coming together, and Coach Spoo had promised that after a year he would get me into NIU. For me, Coach Spoo's word was bond. Like I said before, he was like my football father, a Purdue grad who took a shot on me. I remember down the road, when we were at the coaches convention, they took a picture of twenty-three coaches that had coached under Coach Spoo, all of whom had gone on to be Division-1 football coaches. That is an impressive stat.

Towards the end of spring ball, we all were pretty tired. Backing it all in like this was pretty strenuous. One night, we went to eat and then went back to rest. Just before going to bed, I said to my roommate, Greg Psconda, "Don't worry about answering the phone. I'll get it. I have a feeling Cindy will call and say my son is on the way." At 2:00 a.m., the phone rang. Neither of us answered. The phone rang again, and Greg woke me saying, "Hey, I thought you said your wife was going to call." I answered the phone to find I was right, she was on her way to the hospital.

As promised, Coach got me on the first flight. It was a long journey, 13 hours by plane and car. By the time I got there, Sid IV had arrived. We had just gotten cell phones, so I was able to call while en route. Cindy was crying. "What's wrong?" I asked.

"There are complications, he keeps turning blue," she said. Cindy had prayed every day for a healthy, pretty, smart little boy. She did that with all of our kids. I had been through enough to know that there would be a sign to let me know all would be okay.

I arrived at the hospital, to find Sid IV had been delivered. In this moment, heartbreak and regret would hit me like a ton of bricks. I thought it was all my fault. I should have been there. I should have put my kid first, then nothing would have happened on my watch. I went in to see him and put my finger in his hand. He pulled himself up. The nurse said, "He will be just fine, he is already warrior strong." For me, that was all I needed. Coach allowed me to stay for a week. We moved two practices back so that I could spend more time catching up on schoolwork and spend time with Sid and Cindy. All was good.

After spring practice and recruiting came to an end, as well as completing my studies, I went back to EIU to graduate, pack up my family, and move to the Upper Peninsula. Now, when I left in May, there was still snow everywhere. We got in our U-Haul, hooked our car to the hitch, and began a new family adventure. I warned Cindy to get ready, as she was in shorts and sandals, telling her I doubted she would be needing this type of attire there. We stopped off at her parents and then continued on our way. Thirteen hours later we arrived. To my surprise, the snow on the ground acts like a natural greenhouse. When we arrived, there was no trace of snow. It was like paradise. Cindy thought I had lied to her, just to make it seem bad. I told her, "You just wait and see."

My friend Alli and her daughter Bri came to visit so that they could see our baby boy. It was a great visit. Always good to have my family come around. On her visit, they did some sightseeing. They took a trip out to Pictured Rocks, a place where you could see Native American pictures drawn on the cliff. When they came back, Alli told me how a guy came up to her and asked her what she was doing there. Alli has some fire to her. "Excuse me," she said.

He responded saying, "Sorry, I am from Detroit, and up here, these people are extremely racist."

She told the man that her brother was up here coaching football. He suggested she tell me that I should leave as fast as I can. I told my sister that that seed was planted long before I came.

Racism to this point in my life had played with my mind. I saw every word someone else spoke as my truth. I was ready to begin a shift. As we play victim to the beliefs of others we start to move in a direction that is against our own dreams. In time we all choose where we want to invest our thoughts and begin to make a conscious choice of where we want to go next.

We went into the season bringing in a couple of good recruits. We started off like gangbusters. We were on the hunt to be conference champions. We went to play a powerhouse in Saginaw Valley, a great game we won. Then we would go on to face Grand Valley State, with Brian Kelly, the future Notre Dame University head football coach. We lost that game but had taken a team from a losing record and turned it into a great season at 7 and 3. We just missed the playoff, but it was a great run.

After the game, I went to celebrate with our offensive line coach, Shawn Corbett, at a local pub. I recall joking with the waitress—knowing no joke is ever really just a joke. There is always a hidden truth. I said, "Hey, how about a round of beers for the winning coaches."

She responded, "Let me ask the owner."

He came over and said, "Hey, we don't serve any niggers free alcohol, even if you win a football game."

Corbett was a big dude; he played the offensive line for the San Diego Chargers. All 6'6", 300-plus pounds of him stood up and said, "What did you say?"

I grabbed him, which was unlike me, and said, "Hey, let's just go, it's not worth it." We left. But during recruiting, we went back for a team function. It was like the owner had no clue of the incident. I knew my days were numbered. I was with a great group of guys on the field, yet I knew this was a means to an end.

That year we got 251 inches of snow, a record dumping at the time. I knew I had to get a job. I told Cindy I would get a job at the convention. Her response was telling me that if we were to move three times in a year and a half, she wanted to go live with her parents so she could finish her degree, and she would join me when we could settle in a final location. Cindy was looking out for what was best to get things done, and I felt abandoned. This was the first sign that I thought maybe I need to shift my life a bit. Time would move, and I would see clear in moments to come.

I went to the convention, and as Coach Spoo had promised, I ended up one of finalists for the coaching job at NIU. Coach Joe Novak had the job before the convention, and he said he'd set up an interview if I was interested. We spoke once I arrived at the convention and scheduled a meeting for Saturday morning. As soon as we got off the phone, I called Coach Holms to tell him I had an interview the next day. He suggested we meet for breakfast in the morning to prep for my interview. He was awesome. He made sure I wasn't nervous, prepped me for what he knew about Coach Novak, and off I went.

It was supposed to possibly be a two-hour interview. We were in for about 45 minutes, when Coach Novak said, "Thank you for coming in. Do you have any questions?"

"Well, Coach," I said, "I see you have a board to use to talk football. Can I draw up what I know?"

He responded with a smile, "I needed to know you are a good person, and that is what everyone says about you. If you can't coach football, I am the head coach, and it is up to me to make sure you coach well."

I left feeling that I was just a token interview. Everyone knew the new rules, and I was fitting in with the quota. Coach Holms asked me how the interview went. I said, "I really don't know. It felt great, and all of the stuff you prepared me for, I never got to do. So we will see."

We got back to NMU, and I began recruiting. A couple of weeks had passed and I was beginning to get lonely. Cindy and Sid had left so that Cindy could complete her degree, and I felt like I was on my own, stuck in the tundra. Just when I had no clue how I would get out of the snow, the phone rang. It was Coach Novak calling to offer me a job. I was sooo happy, it didn't matter what was going to be said next.

He said, "I don't know what I can pay you until I hire two other coaches, but if you want it, the job is yours." I was so desperate that no matter how much it paid, I was ready to go. I knew it was going to be more than $6,000 a year. I called Cindy, and she said she would be done with school in six months and would visit on the weekends until then. At this point, I was beginning to harden inside. I started to lose faith in people, tired of facing racism in so many directions.

Time passed and those wounds would start to heal. Just as they would heal, a new one would open. I started recruiting some great players from Michigan and started to bond with my players. I leaned on my relationship with my players to find brotherhood in the midst of feeling like I had to watch over my shoulder. I developed great bonds over the years, with the coaches and friends of old who would continue to help me move beyond the hurt in my heart.

As a kid, I always thought everyone would be love for each other.

Still to this day, I am floored by the conditions people place around their love. If only I had known sooner, how to keep from helping those conditions grow.

At Northern Illinois University, I became one of the youngest Division-1 football coaches. I was 25 years old, and this was also in a time when the NCAA had passed a new law. Every school was now forced to have two minorities on every staff. My best friend Rick, from college, suggested that we both leave the weight room and go on to become graduate assistant coaches. Many will never understand what it takes to walk into a room where five thousand people apply for a coaching job, and you, the young black male, are selected. Life as it was in America at the time had facilitated a story going on in my head, that every day I had to prove myself, that I deserved to sit in that room with so many great coaches. I was fortunate to coach with some of the best. It took me many years to get out of the way and appreciate everything that came from my time coaching football.

The chip that I walked around with as a young coach was what brought greatness out of my players in so many ways. At NIU, we would finish every practice and every game holding our hands up and calling out: "WARRIORS!" You see, I knew, that for me to guide everything out of every player, we had to stand for one another. We had to be willing to leave nothing behind. That is exactly what we did.

In 1996 I was first introduced to yoga when one of my players, Justin McCareins, pulled his hamstrings. We suggested he go take a yoga class on campus. I would always want to know what my players were doing, so I gave yoga a try. Yoga would continue to pull at me for years to come. Although I would not do yoga on a regular basis until 2002, the seed was planted. It was the shift in my body that would give way to my reaching for peace in all facets of my life.

Peace for some truly looks like a restful state, much like being on vacation. I have come to understand that peace for me may not always look like peace on the outside to others. Peace for me is an internal experience, regardless of what may be needed, to bring everything back to the balance of love. A Nahi Warrior is appropriate in action, if and when it allows all to maintain peace in every way inside.

In 1998 Cindy and I were expecting our second child. It is funny how, when we think one thing, something else shows up to help us land and shift our lives. A major shift for me during this year was when I had surgery for a fused right ankle that would slow me down a bit. I coached through spring season in a cast. Boy, was that an interesting journey.

I was told I was the worst patient ever. Dr. Glasgow, our team doctor, decided to schedule to have my cast cut off as a result of my starting the process myself. Heck, after a long, seven-month recovery, I swore I was healed. I was incorrect. Yet, I was healed in my mind. I struggled with feeling out of shape. I lifted so much, my upper body weight made me ridiculously top heavy.

In June of 1998 TD was on his way. I was a football coach, so it was only fitting that his initials came first. I figured I already had a Sid, and I wanted him to know how dear he was to me, so the only option was to call him TD and find names that would fit. Trent meant swift runner, and David is my brother's name, so Trent David it was. He was supposed to be born 10 days after the Michigan camp. It was a Friday, and I was preparing for camp when Coach Novak came into my office. He had this look on his face that had me thrown off.

"Sid, I have to talk to you. Can I come in?"

"Sure, Coach, I am just getting ready for camp."

"Well, that is what I want to talk to you about."

I thought to myself, oh boy—does he know they took me out for my birthday last year? We had some good times at the Michigan Camp, like the time Coach Brady Hoke, Coach Soup Campbell, Coach Mike Mallory, and I would hang out with Tom Brady at the Brown Jug. It was pretty mild, because we had to coach the next day. At least for everyone else, anyway. Soup knew I was hung over, so he did not mind when I would have to excuse myself. Even Coach Lloyd Carr came in and made a joke the next morning about how he heard it was an interesting night. Man, I tell you, these were some of the best times ever. So back to the story: Coach Novak walked in with a serious face and said, "Well, Sid, I am going to have to insist you don't go to camp."

"Okay, Coach. How come?"

"Well, Carroll (Coach's wife) insists that if you miss the birth of another child because of this damn game, I am getting divorced."

Coach went on to tell me how, when he was recruiting, there were no real rules. You would have to camp out, making sure no one else would come by and recruit a player, or they'd take them away from you. He said one day he had been on the road for several days. His kids were home, and he missed them. He was sitting by a tree having lunch, and a song came on the radio: "Cat's in the Cradle," by Harry Chapin. This is a song about a father who neglects his son, but he doesn't realize it until the son grows up and neglects *him*.

I sat there thinking just what a blessing Coach Novak and his wife were to me. He planted a seed in my heart in that moment. That seed landed deep. I know without a doubt that was one of the moments when I became a better man. Funny how even as I write this, I get a little choked up. So much so that I pause in this moment, to call Coach to say thank you! Yep, that is how old ball coaches do it. We pick up the phone.

I must admit, I was a little upset at first. Then when we spent the weekend at the pool, where I got to rest up, and TD was born three days after camp, I was beyond happy. In that moment, I began to see just how much I could love. TD has been one of the biggest blessings of my life—all my kids are. TD is the middle child, and so I always made sure he felt special. I was the middle child, and my mom never wanted me to feel left out, so she treated me as if I were the only child. Meaning: she gave me all the attention she could, to make sure I knew I was a priority in her life. I have special parents, and I wanted to be there the same way for my kids. TD and I have had a huge bond that continues to grow, as he continues to teach me a deeper sense of love every day.

"When I shift, the world around me shifts as well."

My daily routine as I prepared for spring football started in military-strict work ethics, and ended in tequila shots. I woke up one March morning of spring practice the same as usual: bright and early at 4:40. No alarm clock, just self-will. No matter how awful, sick, or hungover, my eyes would crack wide open at a quarter to 5:00. I had my routine down to robotic precision. My bags were packed and waiting at the door from the previous night of preparation. I would look at my wife, sleeping in bed. The next time I would see her, she would be asleep, as well. We could go days without looking each other in the eyes or eating dinner together. I would peer in on my kids to make sure everything was okay, brush my teeth, eat a Spartan-light breakfast, throw on sweatpants and a t-shirt, grab my bags, and be out the door.

The life of a Division-1-A football coach is simple: you wake up and go to sleep thinking about your team. Every day my peers would be trying to find that extra edge, that extra few minutes that would separate them from everyone else. There is only one thing more difficult than getting a major coaching job, and that's keeping it. I was determined to excel at all cost. That determination was my alarm clock every day.

The first signs of light would creep across the sky in dull, gray streaks. I could see the Huskies stadium outside our window. The dawning day made the concrete arena look like a modern Colosseum. Less than a few miles, away it loomed over our backyard and served as a giant monument to competition, brotherhood, and battle. On game day, the roar of the crowd would reach our front steps. I would glance at it every morning leaving and every evening coming home. Even though it was spring practice, the snow-covered fields made it feel like Alaska. Northern Illinois's autumns and springs often became one prolonged experiment in winter attrition. It could be 15 degrees well into April at times. You had to love football to be out this early, braving the Arctic blasts from Canada.

I would gather my thoughts in the car on the way to practice. If I were hungover and struggling, I would pray and say, "If you get me through this, I will stop. I won't do this anymore. I just want out of this. There has to be a bigger job, a bigger something that can bring me happiness." I wasn't thinking that I needed something spiritual. It was about a job and the right connection to my wife. I never thought the problem was needing a deeper connection to spirit. I would pray before meals, pray before bed, but awareness never dawned on me.

Arriving on campus at 5:00 a.m., I would immediately make my way to the gym to work out. Shaking off the morning cold,

I started with cardio. Putting the stair master to the steepest setting, I would blast through a 30-minute warm-up while reading the newest coaching book and listening to Tupac. After starting a sweat, I began throwing my 190-pound frame around with the daily weight-lifting combos, whether it was chest/tri(ceps), back/bi(ceps), legs, or shoulders and abs. Players growled and screamed their way through extensive off-season training.

"If I am happy deep within, keep going. If not, stop digging and get out of the hole."

Even though Huskies football is only played for a few months out of the year, the mental and physical training is year-round. In order to make it through an entire season, our players needed to build a body that was strong enough to take the shock, light enough to keep them agile, and flexible enough to avoid getting shredded in grueling practices and hitting drills. On any given day, the players would break out into specific exercises based on their position. Quarterbacks and running backs would want to focus on strengthening their core. Kickers and punters often came from a soccer background, and so their upper-body strength was always something that could be better. The top-heavy linemen might be improving their agility with the plyometric routine of leaping on to and off of an obstacle course of boxes (in fact, everyone did these grueling plyometric routines).

I coached wide receivers. Hand-eye coordination and quick feet were premium attributes that could be improved in these early-morning workouts. Wide receivers don't take as many collisions as linemen, so they often get teased as the pretty boys of the football team who are off on their own island. If you asked a receiver in a game how it looks out there, nine times out of ten, they'll say the same thing: "Coach, I'm open! I'M WIDE OPEN." I can say that NFL wide receiver image had trickled down into college and high school, with kids who demand the ball and want to emulate players at the next level. That was not the way I coached my receivers to play. They might demand the ball, but they were going to hit, block, train, and grind it out with the toughest lineman. The training helped insure their long-term safety, because they're running at 10-15 mph against a defender who is launching themselves at them with equal speed and force. The shock of these hits are much like a head-on car crash at medium speed. Although they don't hit as much as other positions, when wide receivers do get hit, the potential for concussion or muscle and bone damage is often much greater.

My workouts were just as intense as the players'. I wasn't going to develop that infamous coaching gut during my time on the sidelines. If our bodies are temples, then during my days as a football coach, mine was impressive and well built, with thick walls and a strong foundation.

At 8:30 a.m., I gathered with the other coaches for a staff meeting. We spent the rest of the morning and early afternoon meeting with the players. If we were installing a new play, we would often draw it out, name it, and then do a position-by-position walk through. Most of coaching isn't yelling and motivational speeches. It's teaching young minds how to think tactically and strategically. A successful team instructs their players, not only on their position assignments but on the overall goal of the play, the opposing team's most likely responses, and how all the pieces come together.

Great players are trained repeatedly to make complex spatial, body coordinations and mental decisions in under a second. And these complex and instantaneous reactions have to be achieved for hundreds of plays, each one of which has several different audibles and variations. Playing football is like trying to improvise "Swan Lake" among 11 dancers, while several choreographers scream instructions offstage, and you're facing an opposing team trying to trip, block, and tackle your every move. That's why every victory, every touchdown drive, every play is like a mini-performance. Can you blame kids for wanting to celebrate a touchdown or a sack by dancing? Although most football players and coaches may not have the outward appearance of intelligence, the reality is quite different. So much for the dumb-jock stereotype.

By 4:00 p.m., the Huskies players hit the practice field for warm-up, individual position drills, then offensive and defensive team run-throughs, and then the real fun: scrimmaging.

Offense and defense get game-time simulation of new plays and formations. That day, the frigid wind knifed through our uniforms and gloves. Snow that had been plowed off the field and piled high along the perimeter blew across the yard-lines in icy gusts. Once, the players had to reset because the wind was so strong that it swept them out of formation. After a couple of long hours of making plays and muscle-on-muscle collisions, the defense won, and both the players and coaching staff hustled into the locker rooms to thaw out. The team did not have practice the next day, and the staff did not have to meet until the afternoon, so a couple of the coaches and I made plans to grab some late dinner. I drove home, changed clothes, and met them at a restaurant that gave us half-price food and alcohol. We started drinking immediately.

"Eat, sleep, and drink it. It will come."

We all knew fitness and health, but this was our end-of-week, "don't care anymore," kamikaze mission into the land of fried foods and beer. We exchanged notes from the week while piles of French fries, onion rings, buffalo wings, fried cheese sticks, and potato skins made their way around the table. Then the waitress would bring out platters of battered fish, breaded chicken, and cheeseburgers stacked with thick, greasy patties, onions, wedges of cheese, and a pointless wisp of iceberg lettuce. At the time, I thought eating and drinking this way was a reward for a long week of work. In fact it was a subtle form of abuse and lack of self-care. It may sound "New-Agey" for an American football coach to say this, but junk food is a form of punishment. No one ever feels great after consuming pounds of fried beef, carbs, and a few pints of beer. Often you end up tired, nauseous, and sweating from the amount of exertion it takes for the body to even process all the sugar, salts, and fats. But society tricks us into thinking that engaging in ritualistic fried feasts is our compensation for the weekday stress.

Hours later, we left the restaurant filled with greasy food and beer. It was almost midnight, so some of the guys decided to go home. The rest of us decided they were being wusses and headed to Molly's, a bar owned by a friend of ours nicknamed Daddy-O. Daddy-O would let us come in and drink even after he'd close down and was cleaning up. We repaid him by drinking an enormous amount of alcohol. After a few glasses of Captain Morgan, José Cuervo, Tequila Gold, Heineken, and Foster's Beer, it was time to go home.

This particular weekend, Cindy had taken our sons, Sid IV and TD, to her mother's house. As I sat alone in my spinning living room, I reflected on my day, my month, and my situation. When I looked up, I knew it was time for a shift. I knew that it was time to begin to restructure and reconnect to something deeper. This is where it all began. I looked at the pictures of my wife and two kids, our family trips together, and parties. I could place them by timelines of football schedules, realizing how my life had truly been consumed with football. The faces staring at me looked like they came with the store-bought frames: they were happy strangers. This was not how I wanted to feel at home. This felt like four walls where I slept and kept my stuff. I was free to hang out on campus, drink as much as I wanted, drive with my chin on the wheel, and stagger through the front door in the dead of night. My transformation began on nights like these, when I was left to stare at the shadows on the wall. I realized that I was a grown man living in anger, and this was something no longer acceptable. Something had to change. In many years to come I would later learn how sacred the number four would be in my Native American culture and the way of the Nahi Warrior.

My life wasn't terrible, and to claim so in yogic hindsight would be melodramatic. I loved my wife, my kids, and felt football was an amazing sport. You won't hear that from many yoga teachers, but sports can create great men and women. There is a belief in the New-Age community that all forms of competition are inherently violent, and all forms of yoga are inherently healing. This is a mistake. It is possible to be a football player or coach and live a yogic life. Conversely, it is possible to study the deep teachings of yoga for many years and still choose to destroy the body. Amid any chaos, there is always a solitary island of light that shines within. It is this point of light that offers me a chance to be still and know. In silent solitude, there is always a chance to let the mind run around like an unruly child. It isn't the physical act, but the mental intention that determines the refuge—or rebellion—I get from my actions.

It's very hard to become a yogi if life is great. Some are born to rich parents, surrounded by servants, never having to question the pain of life. For these people, finding true happiness is almost impossible because it is that much harder to wake up from a pleasant dream than an unpleasant one. At the same time, if a person experiences too much suffering early on, then that, too, is equally troubling. Extreme pain doesn't allow room for true interacting with others and growth. There is only the worry of fulfilling basic needs and ending the immediate discomfort. For myself and others, we are the fortunate few. We have just enough pain, just enough pleasure, and just enough awareness to have open hearts and to want more.

I was waiting for a sign my whole life, and this empty living was it. I had hoped for something more dramatic and telling, and I had put off any serious change in expectation of thunderbolts, burning bushes, angelic voices, and parting bodies of water. It was my mind making excuses, to avoid examining myself. I had sat in this quiet, dark living room many times, but on this particular night it was different. The sign I had been waiting for wasn't in action but in its vacuum. Those moments when there is no more running, no more sweating, no more trying to do at the end of the day. When I lay in bed at night staring at the ceiling, sitting quietly in an idle car before going to work, or standing on the field after a hard-fought game. In this, I had a few, brief flashes of realization. Although I arrange them now in a coherent and linear fashion, they didn't appear that way at the time. These brief glimpses of light were enough to lead me to ask for more. They were the guide for my way into a new life.

First, I had all the conditions of happiness but none of the results. I had all the material signs of success—the family, a great job teaching young minds, and loving friends. Yet I couldn't locate any one thing as the reason for feeling dissatisfied, dull, and angry. Sure, I could nitpick at something and had done so in the past. I would get in arguments with my wife, disputes with other coaches, and disagreements with friends. I was trying to correct them, thinking "if only they would be this way, I would be happy." Maybe I had it backwards this whole time. It wasn't, "if only they would be this way, then I would be happy"; rather, "if I was happy, then everything would just be."

Second, my happiness wasn't dependent upon those outside factors. As stated, I had all the material and relational factors that should make a person content. So if the reasons are not *without*, then they are *within*. In my head I was thinking and acting in a way that wasn't making me happy.

Third, if my thoughts determine my mood and my mood is one of dissatisfaction, then I could change them. If I refused to change them, I was either a masochist or hopeless. Since I didn't fit either category, there was hope. If there was hope, then there would be motivation to keep asking questions. There had to be a way out because my life wasn't always like this.

Fourth, if I figured out a way to change my mind, then it wouldn't be random. It took a long time and a lot of hard work to make myself this unhappy. Nothing about my success in life was random. Logically, there would be some work to achieve a better result.

Sports can be a great teaching tool, and I was fortunate to live in that world at the time. Discipline in thought and action was required to get any noticeable results. I began looking at how I used and talked about sports, in its positive and negative light. I had bought into the sports-talk lexicon, which means I had been sold on its thought process, too. Words of *war* and *blood feud* in sports seem to be calling for the extension of anger and outrage. I knew that I had to call for the end of it. As a black man, I saw football as both a vehicle of escape and a possible trap.

"Sometimes getting angry is a higher vibration."

As a brief aside, I want to note that the inequalities we contrive (teams, colleges, divisions, conferences) are just extensions of the ones we construct in the daily world. I can see that clearly now, but back then I was oblivious to this strange tribalism that repeats itself again and again, in sports and entertainment. It's no coincidence that our inability to address gross inequalities in society mirror our fear to talk about them in sports. For someone to say that it's just a coincidence that all the most hated sports athletes in Q Ratings are black men from lower classes, while most of the most loved athletes are white, and that has nothing to do with inequalities and privilege, not only takes an enormous amount of denial and fear, but it suggests that the sports world exists in a vacuum outside of reality. The inequalities never get corrected by anger and often only increase the blindness and rage of the privileged, who only end up hurting themselves. Correcting how we create media images isn't to drag more white men into the hatred column and balance out the rage. And if we cannot admit that inequalities have a lot to do with how we view sports, then the only response is a defensive anger to deny facts and nitpick on personalities of arrogant superstars.

Over 90 percent of adults in US prisons for violent crimes have had unspeakable horrors of rape, abuse, and molestation done to them as children. You would think, logically, that trauma would make them less likely to re-enact it, but it's quite the opposite. The "condemnation process" helps ensure a continued and growing cycle of criminality-victimization-criminality. Is it any wonder that as we get angrier and more judgmental as a society, our prison population explodes, our violence increases, alcoholism and drug addictions explode, and the scandals seem to get worse?

But back to my own situation and that dark living room. I saw that my anger and judgment were making me unhappy. I wasn't judging me, but it was the condemnation of others that got me to this lonely, dark place. Coaches, leaders, and motivational speakers love to misquote the Bible. There is one statement about reaping and sowing often used, because the phrase is from holy words in the Bible and meant to be interpreted by the reader, not as a projection on what others need, but a reflection on what *I* need. So it's more correct to say the application of the phrase in current life is: *I reap what I sow*. It is the same thing repeated in many other spiritual traditions, which is: I can only account for what I am farming and do not know what someone else is sowing in their fields, so it's dangerous to judge them. It's my judgment of what others will be reaping that prevents me from focusing on my field, my mind, and my ethics.

"Find grace when all else fails."

Lord Buddha, Jesus, Abraham all say, to a larger extent, that I have NO IDEA what someone else is thinking or doing in their heart. I can only know what I do and think, and so I MUST forgive because I have condemned others in my own guilt and fear. My wife couldn't escape from this condemnation because it was a mindset that I had taken on over many years of un-thoughtful sports talk.

Competition is fine, but judgment is not mine. Years later, I learned that if I do judge others guilty, then I will assuredly reap what I sow, which is a continued cycle of guilt, shame, and projection. I will reap the rewards of projecting this onto others by having it projected back onto me. Often the phrase "reaping" is used as judgment against others, which is the very antithesis of its true meaning. I can only know the seeds that I have planted and cannot ever know others. Football was also great because it's not "real life," but it replicates the battles of reality pretty well. On the field, I have the chance to compete without hatred, to want winning without lusting for the other person's loss, and to simulate gladiator battle and then shake hands on the field before and afterwards to show it was only a game. We were, are, and will always be brothers. No amount of false divisions, made-up tribes, contrived rivalries, and yes, even scandals, could ever erase that fact. We are all brothers. So do unto others as I would have them do unto me.

But how could I do that in a practical, applicable way in my life? I had to find out. I went to bed committed to change. I had made these promises before, and broken most of them, but this time as I crawled into bed, I knew things would change. Tomorrow would be different.

The next day I had forgotten about almost everything I committed to in my desperation. Of course things don't change just because I demand it. Things change when I begin to change my actions. The weekend drifted by, and then it was Monday again.

My daily routine allowed me to slip back into pre-programmed and robotic thinking.

Coaching football is a way of life—hands down, like no other. You have to own your philosophy and deliver it to others. You are responsible for and counting on people uniting for a cause, and winning because of that cause, no matter what, or be fired in the process. I had studied many coaches, and Coach Gary Barnett of Northwestern University had a philosophy worth getting behind. What really landed for me was how he got the team, family, and community behind everything required to produce a winner. When he first got to Northwestern, the team was dead last in many polls, much like we were at NIU. Coach Barnett came in and hung a banner that read, "CHAMPIONS!" He spent years dedicating himself to speaking to his teams with positive language in order to elevate them through his coaching. He had a rule for his coaches: when we wanted or needed to coach a player for a missed assignment, we had to first say what the player did well, and then how they could improve. He had a way about him that I respected a great deal. From my view, he was the beginning of the new era of elevating players to reach a higher level.

In football, you usually respected your opponent. Yet, no matter what, you were prepared to beat them. In 2000, we knew that we were ready to turn the corner and bring our team up. In the years that preceded this, we had gone through heavy growing pains. We had the nation's longest losing streak in 1998. We were so far off at one point, even David Letterman talked about how bad Ball State University was. We were seconds away from snapping our losing streak in that game, when we went into overtime against his alma mater. They even talked about having us play without cheerleaders because the cheerleading coach had resigned. I talked Cindy into applying for the job even though she had never coached. I assured her that I could help her make sure they had discipline, and she was smart, she could figure it out. She took the job, and we were now, truly, a football family. A football coach, a cheerleading coach, football players, and a cheerleader on the way.

We were ready to kick off the season August 31, 2000,

against Northwestern University. We were not going to face Coach Gary Barnett, as he had moved on to the University of Colorado. We would face Coach Randy Walker and his team instead. We knew with them having a fairly new staff, and with our players coming of age, we were going to be ready. I was praying that our new addition to our family would come during our bye week. This would guarantee I would have the best of everything—and Coach Novak wouldn't have to pay me a visit to my office again.

We bused over to meet the Wildcats, stayed the night before, and woke up ready to go. This was an exciting time. We knew this was the season we could win and move this program forward for all to come. We fought hard. We were engaged in a battle. It took great focus. For me, it was like playing chess. I loved it because you were competing, being your best on any given day. We were in the game and battling for the win. I remember at one point, were were driving to score, when a trainer came up and pulled on my jacket. Now, I signaled the plays in, so I was engaged in every game. I had to coach my players, get plays in, and keep cool. She pulled on my jacket and said, "Coach, I was told that your wife is having contractions and may leave for the hospital." I was pretty intense during games. I looked at her and said, "Go over and tell her, not now. She has to wait." Now, you may laugh. Yet understand, I really rarely joke. She made it through the game and we lost. I won because my daughter came right on time.

All of my kids helped me to see a part of myself that was hidden. Sid IV helped to reveal anger within, and in order to help him find peace, I had to be an example of how we can choose to hold peace in any moment. TD was one who, because of how much he loved, would take on any situation as his problem. I was able to see that I could be a stand for myself and speak up; that by practicing self-love and having a willingness to let people go from my life, who are not moving in the same direction of my desires, is okay. It has been great to see my boys elevate as I have reached for a higher vibration and way of being.

Camille Olivia McNairy was born on September 13, 2000. She arrived during the bye week, and we had four wins and only played two games. We had a great win over Illinois State University (52-0), so heading into the bye week, we all felt great. In coaching we had a saying: a bye week after a win was like two wins. From day one Camille was a beautiful little girl. She looks so much like my mom, which means she looks like me in a lot of ways. Another birth of a new life, a new connection, instantly caused me to reflect on my life, as I have been ever since. I looked first at how could I protect this little girl. I knew what the world could be like for any woman, especially one who was as pretty as my baby girl. I instantly looked at ways I would protect her, ways I could shift to be the example of what she could look for in a man.

My first call to duty was to name people to stand with her in life. Even if that was energetic, I wanted to make sure she had warriors to stand for her. First was Deon Mitchell, a great guy who always had a kind heart. Neon Deon, as we called him, went on to play for the Dallas Cowboys. Second was Justin McCareins, who from day one of his freshman year wanted to find the one he would spend his life with. Justin went on to play for the Tennessee Titans and NY Jets. Third was Darrell Hill, one of the coolest guys around, who went to the Tennessee Titans and the Kansas City Chiefs. And last but not least, PJ Fleck, who was the life of the party, high energy, and loved by many. PJ went on to play for the San Francisco 49ers and Atlanta Falcons.

Because of how close I became with my players, I got to see how my reflection was playing out in each of their lives. Especially the example I had been in relationships, and my relationship to football for them. Through my players and my little girl, I continued to shape my life. It would be many years before I truly figured out the flow in my relationship with Camille. It took me getting to the point of total acceptance, and standing up for myself in moments of our relationship.

I found along the way that somehow, everything that I did was as a negative in the long run. I learned how to see from the eyes of love to know beyond a shadow of a doubt that I was a good dad, and a good guy overall. The more I heal me, the more I see my kids grow into the reflection of love I desire to see. In 2000, I would coach my last season at Northern Illinois University, knowing that I built a foundation for the Warriors to continue. I left with a winning season in the books, three amazing kids, and wisdom beyond my years.

After my experience on the couch in 2000, I knew I wanted a shift in how I was being as a football coach. For me this meant looking for a coaching job at a smaller school. I thought a change in environment would allow me to reconnect with my wife and kids. As the next three years passed, I realized it really wasn't the size of the school that needed shifting. I was looking for a state of peace that I personally was not finding in the midst of coaching football. I had a great twelve-year run during which I met some of the greatest people I could have met, from coaches to players to colleagues. It is a part of my life I will forever cherish because I know how it has shaped my life and created long-lasting friendships that will exist beyond all space and time. The summer before my last year of coaching, I had gotten to a point where I was unable to get free in my relationships, and I had to move on. It was another tough time, and I began to lean on my yoga practice even more to find the peace I was so desperately seeking.

CORNERSTONE THREE
Get in the Flow

By now, you have a concept of what it will look like to get into the flow of the universal game of life. In sports we call it *getting into the zone*. Yes, now is an opportunity to understand it on a level you may have missed. It is a time to feel a flow, find that the zone is accessible first when we understand the concepts, then when we put them into action. There is something inside of each of us that is waiting for us to discover our journey, and allow it to move through with grace.

Know that there are many ways to go into the flow. Here, I want to share one that allows you to grasp the moment where you are and begin to use it to see where you are, how you got there, and how you can use it to get to where you desire to be. The flow of life is exactly what took me from teaching in Annapolis, to breakfast with new friends, and to a retreat in Nicaragua. It all started from a willingness to listen for when it is appropriate to say yes, and to flow from one moment to the next.

The practice of flow is a deeper look into removing resistance from our operating system that we move from, moment to moment in life. As I think about flow, I am reminded of the life of Alaskan salmon and how they flow through the natural stages of their life. From the very beginning, they are born into the stream of life to experience, grow, and return through the cycle of life's moments. Life will take them from streams and rivers in the Alaskan frontier, into the Pacific Ocean, and back again. From the beginning, they are prepared to enter into the world. As a small egg, they reside in the bed of a stream until they hatch and prepare to move through the world, and flow into the ocean of life. The first part of their journey will last a couple of years, until they have moved into their next stage. At this point, the smolts (or juveniles) will stay together as they prepare for their trip to the ocean. Along the way, their bodies continue to shift as they begin to adapt to the seawater. As time passes, they grow into being young adults and head out to swim in the Bering Sea and the Gulf of Alaska. Once full maturity is reached, they will swim back to their original stream or river, and at this point they re-adapt back to prepare for the fresh water, and swim back upstream to prepare to lay eggs and spawn the next generation. This can mean swimming upstream or even leaping up waterfalls. The salmon will do what is needed to continue to move fluidly through every stage, to give way for the next generation. Once the salmon have spawned, they die within a week, where they give way to fertilize the stream or riverbed, creating a nutrient-rich space for the new salmon that are about to hatch.

Take a moment and check in to *you*. What is it you want to learn? No matter what it is, you will need to have discipline to finish it off. Embrace the flow of your life like the salmon; sometimes you will flow over, flow through, and flow around things that come up in life. By allowing yourself space to feel the moment and let the currents move you in the direction of your inner wisdom, you will gain a deeper access to the flow of life.

In my time, I have been able to witness the greatest of athletes perfect their trade. Michael Jordan, Walter Payton, Carl Lewis, Wayne Gretzky, Tiger Woods, and many more, had one thing in common: a laser focus to complete the task at hand. By witnessing great athletes, you can see this level of connection gives access to how effortless it can be. I recall Michael Jordan playing one of the best games of his career, exhausted from the flu. It brought me back to recalling my own moments of playing on the field while sick. There is no wasted energy. You find a laser focus that allows you to be with each moment, as if time has all but come to a halt. In each moment, I have found that it is like having blinders to anything else, and being with only what pertains to what is in front of me.

To access the flow, we must fully come to understand the stages of learning and allow ourselves to move gracefully from one to the next. The first stage of learning as a warrior dives into the moments where you are stuck in a place of not knowing. This space is referred as Unconscious Inability. In this phase, the warrior has no clue that a skill is missing. At some point, someone brings this forward, showing a new skill as a way to lift to new heights and knowledge.

The shift into the second stage happens as soon as a warrior realizes there is something unknown that has revealed itself. The second stage is Conscious Inability. Once we realize we do not know something, we have an opportunity to bring it forward in a way that will lift us into a new ability. Through the space of being open to everything, we then don't even know what we are unaware of, giving way to an opportunity to set new heights.

The third stage is Conscious Ability, when the warrior begins to understand what is missing and looks to gain the knowledge that will allow access to learning a new task. When this stage is entered, a warrior can soon perform without thought. To an outside observer, it may look as if they have it all under control, yet the warrior is in a space of thought—thoughts that are allowing actions to come forward for a desired reality. Once the Conscious Ability stage is reached, a warrior then understands that by thinking or using tools, he or she can accomplish the task at hand.

The ultimate of all things we learn in life is for a warrior to land in the fourth stage, Unconscious Ability. We can reach this with the utmost dedication, with attention to detail, and freedom to land in perfection. When a *warrior* lands in the fourth stage, they lift into a space of deep connection to spirit. Within this connection, they have access to the newly acquired ability, and after other abilities come along, so will full access to the new powers. Once we fully open the doorway to fully be in the flow with spirit, we will come into a space to be filled with *spirit.* This connection will allow us to master our new learning and flow in the mastery of many other things to come.

"I am flowing through life with ease and precision."

As I moved forward with my coaching career, I began to see my connection to my team shift. In training, our team was becoming physically powerful, with great football players. I began to see that if we were truly going to turn around Morgan State University football, a program with twenty-three years of losing behind it, we were going to have to find a way to get more into the mental state of our team. I knew that teaching them yoga and meditation would give me a chance to speak to their souls in a different way.

We went into my final year of coaching football with a mission, to give Morgan State football the first winning season in twenty-three years. It was interesting as I began to come into a deeper understanding that our minds play more of a part in the outcome than our bodies. I recall preparing for a shift with our team. I was ready to take on my position of coaching the receivers, working with the quarterbacks, and lifting them up. I knew that the most important part for me was to act as the Special Team Coordinator, knowing I could impact the whole team and we would win.

"A Nahi Warrior knows, that no matter where you are, you have the ability to impact everyone, right where you are."

We would call this unit the Warriors, and each unit was a different special-forces unit. It was through this phase that I could impact and create the culture of our team. We had a great run in the beginning of the season. Our special-teams units moved from being ranked in the bottom two in our conference, to being in the top two in every category, and ranked in the top ten in the nation on quite a few. We scored points in every game on special teams, blocking points, returning points, kickoff returns, field goals, and fake field goals. We found ways to rest our starters and get the best out of every player on the team.

One of the first wins came against the Towson University Tigers. In twenty-three years, Morgan State University had not beaten them. We were down at half, 10-0, and it seemed like the Morgan of old. We knew we needed something big. Coach Hill had guts and believed I was getting it done. "Sid can we get it?" he asked. "Hell, yeah!" I replied. We went for it out of the gate and got the ball; the momentum was now in our favor. We drove the ball and scored, 10-7 and most of the half remaining. We then pinned them deep on the next kick off. Our defense did a great job and got a safety. We were down 10-9, yet spirits were up. Could this be the first time MSU was to beat Towson in twenty-three years? We got the ball early in the fourth quarter, and John Voroshilin kicked a twenty-eight-yard field goal to give us the lead 12-10. Towson would drive down and score again, 16-12, after a failed two-point conversion. We got the ball back after a big return. Bradshaw Littlejohn, our quarterback, broke loose for a fifty-seven-yard run to win the game 19-16. We were elated, and kids stormed the field. We had pulled it off. This win would start us off 1-0 before losing the next three games.

One of the games that was pivotal along the way was against Bethune Cookman. We had gone out to a gentlemen's club the night before the game. When we returned, we were greeted by our head coach, who had a couple of thousand dollars missing from his room. He came over to our room and accused me and my roommate of stealing his money. I assured him I wasn't a thief and was not in his room. He then let us know that if the money was not returned, we would be fired.

I said, "It's okay, I quit." I knew the game and the season at this point would be lost and I would be okay going forward. This was a game-changing moment for me in my life, as I knew football, and the way I was living in it, was going to have to shift. Later, coach's money magically appeared in his pant's pocket, and we would have a hard time looking at each other. We would go on to coach this game, as I knew the ones really hurt by me quitting would be the players. Bethune Cookman was known for their trickery on special teams, and we would need to match their performance with one of our own to win. We had a punt returned on us and turned it around with a block punt, for a touchdown and a big kickoff return. This game was truly back and forth, and we went onto win 31-24 and headed home. This game, for me, marked a moment when I knew I wanted to move forward with my life.

After beating Bethune Cookman we would go on a run, going from 1 and 3, to a 5 and 5 record. We had one game left against Hampton University. Win or lose, we would have a better record than any team at MSU for many years. Win, and we would have the first winning season in twenty-four years. This was going to be a tough win, yet we were ready to pull out all stops.

We had grown accustomed to doing a mental prep exercise every Friday. I would script a game scenario that we had come to realize was mirroring the outcome of the game. As long as we believed and stayed the course, we would come out on top. On this day I scripted a shoot-out, as they had a potent offense, as did we. We also had our edge on special teams. Our game ended up exactly the way we had scripted it on all phases: offense, defense, special teams. We were down to the last two minutes of the game. Coach Hill felt if they got the ball back, we might surely lose this game. When it came time to punt, I told the players to remember how we rehearsed it. They were going to have to take a time out. We came to the sidelines, and I looked at Coach. I must say, he had some guts to ride this out. "Run it," he said. So we went back out and let them line up. The coach from Hampton was yelling at their players to get lined up. Once they were set, I knew we had them. We needed eight yards for a first down. The ball was snapped to John. He stepped left, bent back to the right, and went for thirty-nine yards to seal the game! He was tackled at the six-yard line. Looking back, had he scored, they still would have had life left. Instead, our offense took a knee, and we went on to win. I recall what that winning did. It allowed Don and I to shake hands and leave it behind us on that field. Coaching was over for the season, but the journey was just beginning.

After football season, I would continue to dive further into my yoga practice, coaching yoga on campus as part of the school's curriculum. I was also teaching a healthful living class and helping others find yoga at our local church. During the off-season, I would continue to teach our players yoga. It really helped for them to become flexible and to be prepared for NFL Pro day. We had guys that could drop 2/10 to 4/10 off of the forty-yard dash time. Vishante Shancoe had done such a great job preparing his body that when he would go on to the NFL combine, he would perform at his highest.

After spring football, I could feel the shift building inside. I was happy helping others and all seemed to be in a great flow. Funny how the universe is playing with us, even when you're not looking. I was in a comfort zone, and something was going to have to push me so that I would make a shift. I was just about to do something out of the box, where the chain reaction would start to take place, to speed up the process of me becoming a full-time *yogi*.

I even went away to study yoga in order to teach our football team. My first yoga training was pivotal in my shift all around. I remember sitting around with everyone, listening to my teacher, Rodney Yee, and being able to ask questions there. At this point in time, football and yoga had no real relation to each other. My first question to Rodney was, "I see you have legs as big as mine, and I squat 500-plus pounds. Do you feel that football players should lift weights?" As soon as I mentioned football, I remember most of the people tuning out. His response would forever shape my yoga practice.

Rodney was sitting in lotus position at the front of the room. He pressed his hands to the ground and lifted up into a handstand, moved down into a side crow, moved to the other side, lifted up into a handstand, came into a one-legged crow, and then the other side. Finally, after what seemed like ten minutes had passed, he landed back in lotus again. "Now," he said with ease in his voice, getting every person in the room's attention, "Can your football players do that?"

My answer was, "Heck, no, I'm not doing that."

"Well then", he said, "They need to lift weights because in their sport they need body armor. Yet they need to be able to move with ease through all challenges, and they will be better players."

To this day, I teach this to athletes. When they come to practice with me, this is one part of developing the Nahi Warrior within. Yoga, life, and sport are all part of our practice for the game we play, daily "living." By being challenged on the mat, we learn the true power of the Nahi Warrior is through an inner peace forged in our daily practice. Life is often challenging. When we learn to operate with peace, all challenges are then shifted into opportunity to move deeper on one's path.

As we continued into the week, I knew I wanted to come up with a question that would stump Rodney. He had such a profound way of answering my question that I wanted to come up with a way of presenting a question that had perplexed me since I was three years old. Over the course of the week, we went through exercises that continued to open me up. I worked on handstands that opened and integrated my spirit. We held poses for long periods of time that challenged my will to be powerful. On the second-to-last day, we came together as Rodney showed us postures to help students with ailments. He asked me to come to the front for a demonstration. At this time, I was still suffering from asthma, and we were looking at breathing techniques and how they would support healing. We went to the wall for a posture called, "Legs Up the Wall" or *"Waterfall."* I was guided into moving my breath into my diaphragm. The release brought me to tears. Rodney asked, "What is going on for you?"

I sat with it for a moment and then responded. I recalled the tougher moments in my childhood, the physical movements, the mental stress. I knew it was all flooding up as I shared my pain.

Rodney's response would shift my perspective. He pointed out how most people could not stay with or in the tougher postures, such as Warrior II or Triangle, like I did. He said that my abilities to be with pain was a gift most would never understand. This awareness would help me as time would pass. After this release I felt easy, and my final question began to surface.

We went to dinner at a little sushi sestaurant in Woodstock. It was awesome. One thing that stood out for me beyond the food was the loving care of everyone there. I can remember praying over my food and it being the only time ever in my life when the waiter paused and bowed his head in prayer with us. I thanked him, because I knew the depth of care he had just put into his service. At the end of dinner, it hit me. I knew just how I wanted to deliver my question that had been with me for as long as I can remember. Now I felt like I could go back to training and know that this last day would complete the training for me fully.

Here we were on the final day. We had a great morning practice where I continued to open my body and dive deeper into my heart. Once we had completed our practice, we were called to bring forward any questions that needed to be answered. I was ready to ask, just not sure I wanted to hear his answer. His answer before was so on point, I had nerves coming forward, as I knew there was a chance my life and my walk would have to shift. Ultimately, I would have to make a conscious choice as to where my life would go.

I lifted my arm up to say I had a question. I was amazed, as it seemed as if all the mats had shifted, so that there was a direct line of sight from me to Rodney. He acknowledged me saying, "Sid, you have a question?"

I replied, "Yes, I do. Can I give a little background here, so you can fully understand this question and what it means to me?"

"Yes, please do," he graciously replied.

"Well, at three years old I remember sitting in church. I grew up Catholic, and this was the first time I can remember seeing a symbol of Jesus on the cross. I embraced his teachings and knew that if I were to be the best I could be, I would have to reach for being Christ-like in this life. I went on for years to watch people in the home of the church be mean, be racist, hurt others, and be less than love."

I began to cry as I stated that these actions witnessed over the years is why I have chosen to worship on my own. "It has been through the practice of yoga that I now see how a man could become Jesus Christ. So my question is, could a man have existed like Jesus and have done all of the things he has said he has done?"

His response was so solid, no question in his heart, from my view. He did not hesitate to say, "Yes!" Emphatically, "Yes." He said, "I have seen men walk on fire, walk on water, turn apples into oranges, and more." He said it was not what tricks Jesus could do that made him, it was that even though he could do everything possible, he chose to walk with men.

I knew right in this very moment it was time for me to walk my walk. To open up and be the example I wanted to be for the world. As we closed, I had a card I would give to Rodney to say thanks. As I sat down to talk with him, he said, "You know, you have some of the strongest practices in here, because of the stillness inside of you. Postures have little to do with it, you have more inside than most I have seen."

I was humbled, and wanted to follow him and be his student. He told me that I couldn't, because I had so much to do for the world that I needed to be fully me, because that would change the world.

We parted with him saying, "Get on your mat every day, and let it teach you."

I said thank you and went on my way. My time with Rodney Yee will forever be remembered, as I am grateful for all that has opened up in me since our time together. I am grateful we crossed paths and that I am doing *me* each and every day.

Just before the combine, I went to Pittsburgh to recruit. I stopped into a studio called Amazing Yoga. I remember after the class, we were lying in savasana as Karen, the teacher, was singing. I swore I heard angels as she sang. I went up to her after and asked her what song she was singing. She told me it was by a guy named Krishna Das.

I had to go straight to Barnes & Noble and figure out what this artist was about. The first CD I bought had a song called "God Is Real." I stayed in my room for hours playing the song over and over and over again. This song would open my heart up. I would cry, I would shake, and I would laugh at myself. I knew something was going on, and I just wasn't quite sure what.

I called home to my girlfriend, who would later become my second wife, and told her about this class I took, about this teacher who taught in the same style we did. I told her that the next time I came to Pittsburgh to recruit, she needed to come with me to take this class. The following week, we went back together. We would sit after class with Karen, and she would tell us about her teacher, Baron Baptiste. As coincidence would have it, he was going to be in town in February. We could come and see if we really liked his style. We went home and registered for his course that would take place three months later.

One spring afternoon, we were playing basketball as a staff. We were getting pretty competitive, and the score was tied up. I wanted to make a big play, a big steal that would help us take the lead. I went to take the shot, jumped, and landed on my ankle, twisting my knee in the process. The timing was crazy, as my girlfriend and I were getting ready to take a trip to Arizona. On the plane, I would travel with my leg across her lap after being told I had torn my MCL. It was this trip that would set the stage for a new way in being for me.

My girl and I had a great time on this trip, despite my injury. She was there to study meditation. There was a woman there named Dr. Susan Taylor. She would help me come to understand how I could heal myself. Dr. Taylor insisted that if I took the time to visualize what I was wanting to happen, and if I got active with it, I would begin to feel the shift. I recall getting on the stationary bike, where I would ride for hours, and I would visualize a frayed rope coming back together and my knee began to respond, feeling as if it were a rope mending. It was later that night that I would feel like someone was drilling in my knee and putting the pieces back together. The next morning, I woke to even more pain. Yet, I repeated the process going even further. I got into the pool and allowed myself to move and imagine the healing. I began to feel better. Later in life, this would show up as a way for me to help my body in its own healing process.

The next day, I took a walk, and as I was walking down the street, I noticed a bookstore that had Buddha statues in the window. I went in and began to look around. A woman behind the desk greeted me and said, "Hi there, you seem like someone our local seer would love to meet."

Now, mind you, I was a football coach and had no clue what this meant yet. I was open to having the chance to meet her. "Okay" I said.

"Can you come back at 2:30 p.m.?" she asked.

"I think so," I replied. Since my girlfriend was in her training and I was going to be alone, I decided to go back. Upon my entrance, I was greeted with, "My long-lost friend Sid!"

I had this look on my face of awe, as I had no clue how this lady knew my name. Aleyah Eysesafar was her name, and she said, "You have no clue who you are do you? My lost friend Sidharta."

Still this just wasn't registering for me. Being a person of few words initially, I just went with it. She invited me to the back to sit for a reading. She had cards on the table that she would use for the reading. She looked at my hands and said, "I will not need any of these things to tell you about you. Are you okay with that?" I nodded yes.

She started, "So here we go. I have four for you, four for you to know about yourself. Number one: you are an indigo child. Number two: your son is a crystal child. Do you know what that means to be an indigo child?"

"No, I don't," I said.

She went on, "Well, you were here to pave the way for him. He will go on and help shift the world, so it's up to you to show him the way. Number three: You are going to write a book. A book around 135 pages. This book will go on to change the world. People will read it, and their lives will shift, even if you haven't met them. And the last thing that I need to tell you, number four: you are going to change your profession."

In my head, I thought she was crazy. I knew I would coach into the grave. Coaching was what I was meant to do and ready to do, for the rest of my life.

In that moment she looked at me and said, "Well, I was going to say you'll leave in three days, but since you're going to fight it, it may take you up to a month."

I thanked her for her time and went on my way. Funny thing is, a few years later, I would go back and try to find Aleyah, only to find there was not a bookstore in Scottsdale Arizona that resembled the same place.

On our way home on the flight, I received a text message just before takeoff. The text message said that our head coach was concerned that I left to go on an interview. Normally in the past, I would have gone to the NFL combine. But this time, I chose to take a vacation in Arizona. I was prepared for what was to come in the staff meeting that was scheduled for the next day because of this text. As we started the meeting, I realized that our head coach wasn't there. It was explained to us that he was going to hold the staff meeting on a conference call. This was something I had never witnessed before by him, or any head coach I worked for before.

We went through our regular staff meeting agenda and everything seemed to be okay, and then at the end he asked, "Is Sid there?"

I said, "Yes, I'm here."

He responded with, "So where were you over the weekend?"

"I was where I said I was, on vacation in Arizona." I replied.

"Why do people think you were at the NFL combine?" he said.

"I'm not sure exactly, maybe there was someone there that looks like me. All I know is, I have my plane ticket here because I was told that you were questioning where I was." Because I was very reactive still at this stage of my journey, I didn't give him the opportunity for him to threaten to fire me if he found out I was at the combine.

We got off the phone with things never settled for me. The other coaches tried to calm me down, but the fire was burning inside. I began to plot what I was going to do to leave. I went through our regular meetings covering everything for the special-teams playbook. As soon as six days passed, I was set to walk out the door and walk away from the game I loved. I'd spoken with my girlfriend and decided I was going to become a full-time yoga teacher. So the journey continued.

I went on to leave football a few days later. I knew I had a mission, and it was to teach yoga and build something. I didn't even really know what was to come. I finally resolved, to the knowing in my heart of hearts, that I wasn't cut out to stay in the game or the way I was living in the game. I had already walked away from my first marriage, questioned how I was as a father, and here I was questioning what we were doing with these young men. I knew I could build something that would impact lives for the better. This excited me. I could build my team around helping others. I could create whatever my heart desired. There were others who doubted me, so many people telling me it would never work. It was 2004, and yoga was still a hidden gem. I knew exactly what it was doing to me, and I could see that so many others needed it. I could see the physical benefits and what it did for my players. I could see that it gave people hope. I could see that it would give so much more. Making this move seemed inevitable.

For the next year, we would begin to build our first studio. We started off with the studio in the Broom Factory, an old warehouse in Canton, Maryland, in 2004. It was a lot of fun. I was teaching a lot, yet it never seemed like work. I loved to get on the mat as much as I could and practice with others. Rodney told me that if I really wanted to do yoga, I needed to get on the mat and study *me* to really see how the practice would impact me. I began to develop new tricks, to develop my own way of warm-ups. There was still the part of me that was a coach, and it was this space that would allow me to coach others. I would use the same principles to challenge myself. I always wanted to do and experience what my players did. I would carry this into my yoga teaching as well. I always wanted to grow as a football coach, and I still want to grow as a yogi.

We grew fast over the next couple of years. We moved all our classes into the warehouse, and out of the church. We also moved and bought a house downtown. The shift kept coming and we soon got married. We were making quick shifts in our life, building fast and maybe, a little too fast. One mistake we made in the midst of it all was losing our initial clientele. We didn't realize they wouldn't make the truck from the suburbs to downtown. So as we looked for a new house, we had wiser choices to make. We started looking downtown and ended up buying a place in Towson, as well as building a second studio in Towson. This was a real challenge. I ended up teaching twenty-six classes a week. This was a heavy load and began to speed up the journey quite a bit.

In 2006 we had signed up not only for an event in Washington, DC, with Baron Baptiste, but also signed up for teacher training in Hawaii with him. We figured we needed a honeymoon, so why not do both at the same time? The first training in DC was great; I felt connected to Baron. He had worked for the Philadelphia Eagles and seemed to be a guy's guy.

I recall after our first break, he asked what we thought of the practice. There was a young woman who stood up to complain. She said the practice was really easy and that she thought it would be much more than that. For some reason I felt an immediate sense of protection kick in. He asked if anyone else had any comments to her response.

I raised my hand, and they handed me the microphone. I said, "Well, as a football coach, I understand that any practice is my practice, that if I don't push myself then I will never feel challenged. So if the practice was easy, then maybe you can take in more accountability for your own practice." I have since learned how my Earth self would kick in and defend my ego. There wasn't much love in my temperament back then. I recall Baron looking at me, as if he knew we were going to have a pretty good run together. As years would pass, he and I both would shape each other in ways that we may never even understand.

"When one learns to be a warrior, one must also learn to run." -Hawaiian Proverb

Not even a month had passed, and we were getting set to head to Hawaii. This was going to be an amazing moment for me, a chance to watch my own personal growth accelerate like never before. The next ten years of my life would prove to be the birth of my highest self. We had a couple of planes that we had to catch from Washington DC, to the big island of Hawaii. We sat next to a man who was from India on the first flight. He and I had a great conversation. He asked what I did and I told him that we owned a yoga studio and that we were heading to a training to become better yoga teachers. He was amazing; he was very inquisitive. He wanted to know the business side of what we were doing. So he said, "In thirty seconds or less, tell me what you do."

I began to explain what we did. I think it took me more like two minutes.

He said, "That was pretty good. Have you ever been asked that before?"

I replied, "No, usually I just say what we do, there is no time limit."

He said, "If you can get it down to thirty seconds, you will be able to keep people engaged."

So that was one thing that really shaped me in that moment. I wanted to be able to deliver, so that people could hear, what we were doing. He then went on to tell me that the biggest secret he had in his life was to always remember to play like a child. To just have fun with life, to enjoy what you're doing so that it never becomes work.

Looking back on it, it was like that flight was ordained by God himself. I then took out my journal and began to write. I began to write questions down that I would ask people I would train in the future to become yoga teachers. I would write descriptions for each posture and how they could each teach a lesson. It was in this moment that I committed to being more detailed in my delivery and in how to make what mattered most relatable in thirty seconds or less, while impacting someone for the better.

On the second flight, my wife and I began discussing different things about life and yoga, where we see ourselves now, and what we might want in our future yogis. We discussed questions for a teacher-training application. The big one was: if you could have dinner with six people, who would they be and why? I named five really quickly, and I can remember my wife stating I had no women. I said, "Well, no, I don't. I am saving the sixth spot for her." I could make it easy and talk about Jesus's mother, Mary. And there was my mother, too. I could talk about Mother Theresa, and that also seemed too easy. Some time would pass, when all of the sudden, it came to me. I wanted to sit with Joan of Arc. She let man know she was a warrior, and it intrigued me to know what it would be like to be that powerful.

Once we got settled at the Ramashala, the retreat center down the street from where we were doing the training, we decided to take a walk to Kalani, where we would complete the training. On our way, I stopped when I saw a huge hawk sitting in a tree. It was only about nine feet in the air, very close. I stopped and stared at this hawk as it stared back at me. It was like it was exchanging energy with me in such a familiar way, as if we were kindred spirits and meant to share each other's company. I stood there, locked in this beautiful moment with this magnificent creature for quite awhile, until my wife eventually asked, "Are we going to go?" As we started to walk, coming towards us was a red, old Sanford-and-Son-type pickup truck. It was an old, beat-up red truck, with palm tree leaves hanging out the back. When he pulled up, he came to a stop. The truck was going in the wrong direction, at least from the direction we were walking. The guy rolled down his window, leaned over, and asked if we wanted a ride.

We just got off a plane, this guy is going in the wrong direction, and we know no one in Hawaii, so it seemed pretty simple to decline. He laughed and said, "You know, you seem like a guy who's connected to nature. You will probably see whales today." We said our goodbyes, and he was gone as quick as he came. We weren't quite sure what he meant by his statement. We continued along on our walk.

Once we arrived at the Kalani Resort, we decided to have lunch. It was really nice just to be able to sit outside and feel the warmth of the sun, as the air was so crisp on the walk over. You could smell the orchids hanging on the trees. It was shaping up to be a wonderful first experience on the island and the perfect start to what I knew was to be a great week. As we walked back from lunch, it was nice to walk along the cliff's edge. I remember we were both facing west, when all of a sudden, I grabbed my wife's arm and pointed to the water. Just then, three whales came leaping out of the ocean. She said, "How did you do that?" I really have no clue. I just know I pointed, and they came up. There was something to it, I just wasn't sure at the time.

We got plenty of sleep the night before our first day of training. The first assignment was to come to the microphone, say your name and where you're from, and two things you wanted to shift about yourself. When I finally got up to the microphone to introduce myself, I knew I had one thing to share. I said, "I want to let go of anger," and said I wasn't sure what the second one would be. Baron then challenged me.

He said, "There must be a second."

I replied, "No, I don't think so. I can make one up for you if you'd like. I just thought you wanted us to be real. And at this moment, I only have one."

He then said something that struck a chord with me.

My earth-self immediately went to racism. Now, I am pretty sure I was the only African American in the room, so my thoughts were that he was asking because I was black. I said, "Yes, I know my father. He's a great guy, he's been in my life, all of my life." So here, my normal pattern of butting heads with my friends was now taking place with Baron. It seemed to me that we stood there for way too long, debating what would be the second thing. To this day, I still shake my head, and couldn't even begin to tell you what it was we settled on. I just thought we were in for a long week. I knew me and that four-year-old that didn't want to give in—and wasn't ready to give in now.

We learned a lot that week. We learned about sequencing yoga practices, assisting yoga practices, looking at ourselves, and understanding our inner child. All of this work began to hit me deep in my heart. There were times I even challenged the group, only to realize I was making the same mistakes in my life, as well. I must point out that we had an intense daily practice while we were there. I swear, it was like we were practicing for four hours at a time. It was a great practice. We held frog for twenty-five minutes, and I can remember how open my hips got. Everything in my body felt better during this practice.

As we laid in *savasana*, I could feel my heartbeat pounding out of my chest. It was beating so hard and loud I thought everyone around me could hear it. All of a sudden, it went from pounding to nothing at all. Right then and there, I really thought I may have died. I didn't want to open my eyes, for fear that if I opened my eyes, I would confirm that I was dead. So I laid there for what seemed like an eternity.

Then all of a sudden, I heard this huge BOOM! My heartbeat came back stronger than ever. It was a consistent pulse, like the beating of a steel drum. I felt electric, as if electricity were coursing through my whole body. I felt truly alive.

We then sat up and began to om. They continued to play music, and the next thing you know, we were dancing. Dancing like nothing else mattered. As I moved around the room, it seemed like everyone was watching. At one point, I made eye contact with Baron. We ended up dancing towards one another. By the end, we were in the middle and everyone was dancing around the center circle. We ended up hugging, with everyone joining in to create one huge hug around us. It seemed odd for a football coach to be here now, and yet it seemed perfect.

We had an extra day layover after the training finished. We returned to the Ramashala. Bhakti, the caretaker, was eager to have dinner first. She wanted to show us how she would cater a meal if we wanted to bring people to a retreat in Hawaii. As we sat down for dinner, the conversation was great. We talked about her, her life journey, and how she became the caretaker of this land. Towards the end of the evening, I asked her if her name was always Bhakti? She said no, that her name was originally Joan, and that she was named after Joan of Arc. This blew my mind! Here I said I wanted to have dinner with Joan of arc and here we sat, in perfect synchronicity. I learned so much that night, and so much from this journey that had just begun. I was truly excited for all that was to come.

In June 2006, we chose to continue our studies with Baron, aka "B," as I nicknamed him, as I often do the fellas I rely on. It took my going to Montana to have my first experience of a ceremony of my people. During this next training, I would experience my first sweat lodge. Here, I was with Native American blood. Later, I would learn that this was far from the tradition of my people and was a profound experience nonetheless. I had to accept the healing that I had done on my asthma and begin to face the fear deep inside of myself. This is where my journey took an entirely new turn.

At the completion of this training, we came home and discovered a deeper space and adapted our meditation practice that would take us further down our path. We were in our new house for about six months, and now had the space to meditate.

To sit, and see, just what was possible in this practice of finding stillness. One night my wife started breathing really heavy. Her breath was so loud that I began to open my eyes just to see what it was I was hearing. She began to make movements that threw me off. She even turned her head so far around, I started to feel nervous. I told her that I thought we needed to stop and see if we could find someone that could help us understand what we were going through. She began to laugh hysterically and uncontrollably. This threw me off even more. I became concerned, as the only thing that came close to what I was witnessing was something straight out of a movie.

The next day, a doctor came to the studio. She was a student of ours for quite some time. When she came in, she addressed us in a manner that was a little different than normal, as if she already knew something was different, that something had transpired. We told her of the experience we had the night before, and she said, "I think you need to meet my spiritual teacher."

We ended up setting an appointment to meet this woman, in hopes that she would be able to guide us further along this journey. In the meantime, we decided to try meditation again, knowing that everything was okay. My wife would start with her breath again. This time I could feel a heightened sense of energy in my own body. She actually began to move around me in circles, faster and faster and faster and faster. She was sitting in lotus position with her legs connected and was rocking in the same position all around the room. I sat still with an awareness of what was happening.

She came back in front of me and jumped to her knees. I was not prepared for what would come next. She bowed, then looked me in the eyes, and bowed again.

I asked her, "What are you doing?"

She grabbed my shoulders and said, "Be quiet!"

I started to speak, and she said it again, "Be quiet! We are here to speak to you. We are here to guide you."

Now mind you, this was my wife. My wife who I meditated with, ate with, and spent my days with. And now she was talking to me as if there were people talking through her. They went on to say that they were the universal council, and that they were here to help me remember who I was.

This went on for days, with moments to speak and listen. I'd listen to the guides that were trying to communicate to me. I would learn so many things. They spoke of love and how love is a simple connection to the source of all things. They defined love as the connection of your reflection to the source. It was amazing to have this contact for the first time, leaving me baffled and astounded, yet grateful at the same time.

My meditation journey would continue to unfold in several ways. I once moved through a yoga practice where my body seemed to control itself. I would move through this practice and watch, as if I were witnessing how my body needed to move, in order to be open. I still use some of these movements today when I'm teaching, to help others find an opening for themselves. There are times I would lie in bed, and something would hold down one side of my body and stretch out the other side.

From my view, this is where we are in yoga today. We use yoga postures to open ourselves up to the energy that's inside. In the past, yoga was used to stay open. You would be meditating, and as the energy needed to move, you would move. Humans are now further away from the source; yoga practice can take us in another direction. We can get back to being connected and spend time listening through meditation.

I would learn a lot from the spiritual teacher that we were introduced to through our student. She taught me about my reflection and how it worked in seeing others as myself. She helped me to understand why we are here and how we picked our parents for the lessons we needed in this life. She helped me to understand much of the ancient text and how my experiences have mirrored what was said.

In the end, I walked away knowing that I was meant to go live my experiences, and that knowledge would serve me to evaluate what I had experienced. I appreciate all my time with all the teachers I've ever had. Each of them has provided me a deeper look into myself and a deeper understanding of who I was meant to be in this lifetime.

In April 2007, I met one of my most profound reflections. It wasn't until I met this miraculous teacher that my life really did change. She goes by the name Jeanne Katz, among other names such as Grandmother Morningstar. I would come to call her "my grandmother." I met her just before my life was about to be turned completely upside down.

My wife and I were set to make a trip to attend the Omega Institute conference in New York City. The conference was called "Being Fearless." We were going there to help support the yogis and to assist the yoga teachers and speakers in leading their parts. We had an argument the night before we were supposed to leave. It was so intense that when we got back to the house, we decided not to go.

I can remember this huge storm blowing in that night. My wife went to the bedroom, and I lay on the couch. Outside of the window, we had this oak tree that stood about twenty feet above our house. I knew by the way it was blowing that if the wind blew it hard enough, it would fall on our house and create major damage. I began to watch the storm. It was already late, probably around 2 a.m.

As I watched the storm, something said to me, "This storm is inside of you." I began to see that I could slow the storm down in my heart. Funny thing was, as I did this, the wind began to slow down as well. I slowed it down until it seemed like there was almost no storm at all. I thought, this can't be true. I can control the storm? So I thought if I can slow it down, I can speed it up. So again I thought about the argument, and as I began to get madder and madder, the storm picked up. I slowed it down again, then I picked it up, then slowed it down. I truly felt connected to nature in this moment.

So now, a couple hours had passed, and I figured I'd better get some sleep. I made sure to calm the storm down inside, in hopes that the storm on the outside would stay calm as well. When I woke up the next morning, it was sunny and the tree had survived the night. I was clear on the inside, and everything seemed clear on the outside. I heard my wife in the shower. I went in and asked if everything was okay. She replied, "Yes, I'm going to head up to New York. Are you going to come?" I told her if we could ride together without fighting, that I was in.

We actually had a pretty good trip up. We checked into our room and would get our assignments the next day. While we were there, we got the opportunity to listen to Jane Goodall speak on her journey in the jungle and her life with the apes. She was amazing. She would demonstrate her chimpanzee calls. They were so loud, if you closed your eyes, you felt like you were in the jungle alone with them.

The next speaker spoke about global warming. We sat for a while and both started feeling very tired. We decided to get up and go look at the exhibits of jewelry, clothing, food, you name it. As we walked through the exhibits, I noticed a table with Native American jewelry on it. I had been seeing so many hawks since Hawaii and wanted to get something to remind me of them. It seemed as though they were connecting me to my heritage. I spoke to the lady working there; her name was Gemma. I asked her if she had any jewelry with hawks on it. She said that they often did, but she wasn't sure if they brought any with them this time. We looked around the tables and we couldn't find anything. She then looked up and asked, "Why do you want something with the hawk?"

I went on to tell her my story of how hawks are with me all the time, how I saw them driving up, and how I see them almost every day. Typically they were red-tailed hawks, but sometimes they were peregrines, or goshawks. I shared how I had an innate sense that they held a message for me.

She seemed to pause and then proceeded to say that the elder of the land was here and knew that I was coming. She said she was off listening to Al Gore speak at the moment and that I should come back tomorrow to meet her. She then again asked me about why I wanted something with a hawk. I gave her the same answer. She then went to her purse and said, "I have a pouch with hawk feathers that I brought for you. You need to pick out four feathers and meditate on their healing for you." I was much obliged to take the feathers, and we left for the night.

At the end of next day, we came back to meet Jeanne Katz, the elder of the land. When we met, I felt an immediate connection.

She was busy, so we had to come back later, but something happened in that moment. I felt a spark of sorts ignite in my body. At the base of my spine, there was a new vibration. It was a deeper sense of the same energy shared with the first hawk in Hawaii, and the many more that followed. Something was awakening within me. I would later learn that this energy was that of a kundalinI rising.

That evening at dinner, I asked my wife if her phone was ringing? She said, "No, why? What do you mean?" I explained how I kept feeling this vibration under me, and I thought maybe her phone was the cause of it. She pulled her phone out and laid it on the table.

The vibration continued and would continue for many days to come. At one point, the vibration and the energy within got too intense. I was in the middle of assisting Sean Corne in a workshop, and I told her I needed to go and find the little Native American lady. I felt she was the only one that could explain what was happening.

When I found her, she walked up to me and hugged me. It felt as though a surge of electricity entered the crown of my head and flooded through my body from head to toe, back up to my head, and down and up. It did this four times. Then all of a sudden I began crying hysterically and laughing at the same time. I was cold and I was hot, I was sweating and I had the chills.

Jeanne took my hands in hers, looked in my eyes and said, "It will all be okay."

I chuckled and said, "I know it will, but this all so very strange and different to me."

We sat down and talked. She said, "Tell me something about yourself."

I told her I had been looking for answers my whole life. My ancestry is African American and Irish, and I know that I have Cherokee blood, but I don't know that much about that side of my family. I told her that I felt that the hawks were bringing me information, that there was something significant that I needed to know. Then I started to shake uncontrollably and cry.

She gently held both my hands and said, "The hawk calls us to a deep level of the unconscious to remember who we are. The hawk tells us that everything is ready to be cleansed of all that we no longer need. The hawk is the messenger that tells us that we need to wake up. It is powerful medicine when it shows up on your path. Your life is about to change."

Then she invited me to a sweat lodge she was having on her land and gave me the pouch with the rest of the hawk feathers. We exchanged information and said we would get in touch soon. Heather and I packed up our car and headed home..

Two weeks later, I came home and half my house was gone. My wife had left, and my life turned completely upside down. She left me a note. The note read, "Go and find that little Native American lady, she is your guide."

The next day, I got an email in my inbox from Jeanne Katz telling me about the sweat lodge. I called her, filled with heartbreak and confusion. She helped me to stay with love instead of anger. She helped me stand in the fire of what was happening to my life, to let go of reacting, and to witness it all with compassion for us both. She helped me stay in my peace, in a moment of intense emotion.

Meeting Jeanne was like coming home. They say that when the student is ready, the teacher arrives; and from the very first moment I saw her, my body, mind, and spirit knew that I had found my teacher. Many years later, Jeanne was interviewed about our first meeting. She told the reporter that she knew in that moment my world would never be as it was before. But I am getting ahead of myself.

Before I met Jeanne, I had already traveled a long road towards my self-discovery. I had left the world of football coaching and discovered yoga through astounding teachers like Rodney Yee and Baron Baptiste. My first marriage had dissolved, as had much of my anger, which had been a part of me since the beginning. I had forgiven my father for his beatings and understood that, despite his harsh discipline, he was a loving father. I took ownership of my own anger to heal us both.

Jeanne had given me an assignment. She said when you come up for the sweat lodge, grab some tobacco and some red cloth. Every time you think of something you want to shift in your life, take a pinch of tobacco, pray for it, and put it in the pouch. So as I drove up to the sweat lodge, I did just that. By the time I got there, there wasn't much tobacco left in this tin. Upon arrival on the land, I went to the house and asked if Jeanne Katz was there? They said she'd be out in a second.

Now the first time I met her, I saw a tiny Native American lady who looked like my grandmother. When she came out of the house, she was a tall, blonde-haired, blue-eyed white lady. I was blown away and thought someone was messing with me. I really didn't think it was she; I was dumbfounded as to what was taking place. Had I lost my mind in New York? Or was I losing it now? Had I really made her into something that was not real, or had I connected to what I was seeing in spirit? I mean, my grandmother had passed on, and I missed her. I had written my grandmother every week in college, and I loved the connection we had. This would be exactly what I needed to move me forward. I needed love, kindness, a caring hand to move me beyond where I was now.

We then prepared for the sweat lodge, and boy did I work hard. I swear I did every job possible. I tended to the fire, I helped gather stones, I helped with the spirit path, I helped create a collage, and I even carried the water that was to be poured during the sweat. It was great. I learned so much that day. It is a Native saying that if you were going to take on a tradition, you better pay attention because it isn't passed along in books. It's passed along through the heart. On this day my heart would be opened wide for what was to come.

As we prepared to go into the lodge, I was told that I would carry the stones, which was fine by me. What was a little more work? We all entered the lodge, set the stones, and it was time to begin the first round. Jeanne asked to have the door closed, when I stopped her and said, "I made a mistake. I'm not supposed to be here."

She said, "What do you mean?"

I could feel myself closing off, feel my heart pounding away. I felt scared deep inside. I was scared of what was going to happen.

She said, "Well, you see those two big guys I sat next to you, they're going to make sure you stay."

I had nothing to say. I didn't know these people. I didn't know what was to come next and figured I'd sit there and see.

During the first round, my heart was racing. The energy that was coming up was nothing short of ginormous. I felt like it was going to knock me down every time I took a breath. I dropped to my knees and bowed, bowed to the ground. We sang and continued through the round. More water was poured onto the hot rocks and the sweat was pouring out of me. As the round came to an end, I felt better and seemed to be okay. Jeanne asked how I was, and I said I was okay.

Then came time for the second round. I went outside to help gather more of the hot stones from the fire. We brought them in and placed them one by one. It seemed like it was going to be an easy round. As soon as the door began to come down and the heat slowly enveloped us, I felt the fear again. My heart was pounding, the energy was flowing, and I felt like I was going to be put down on the ground again, except this time all the way through the ground. I felt overwhelmed. I knew I wanted to get out. Yet, I knew they were not going to allow it. I thought to myself, how can I get through this again, and two more times after this? The energy continued to move through me. I made it through the round and sat up before they opened the door. It was pitch black in there with the door closed, and somehow they knew I was down again anyway.

"Are you okay?" she asked.

I replied, "Yes, I'm fine. I just don't understand why I'm so overwhelmed. I'm not sure what I'm supposed to do."

On the third round, I went outside to help gather the stones again. Kevin the fire keeper was kind of laughing and serious at the same time. He said, "You'll be okay."

I said, "Yeah, I know, just feeling off."

We took the stones in and the door came down. You betcha, I felt the panic set in again, this time more than the last. I felt like something was trying to get out of me. Something wanted to show itself, and I had no clue what it was. The round went on, we sang again. At the end of this round, when the door would open, it was a water round. As she passed water around, people got to share what they were feeling.

I was still in the midst of the energy of spirit. I still felt overwhelmed in my heart. I couldn't catch my breath. Something was coming up, and I just wanted to let it go. One of the elders spoke to me and said, "I've seen you before. It's always the prophets that have the toughest time on the first lodge. You have a lot of work to do here, and it's going to be tough on you, but you can handle it, because it's what's meant to be. It'll be okay."

Her words gave me some life. I felt a little stronger, and then Jeanne spoke. She said, "Look around, "Grandson," everyone in this sweat lodge is older than you are. They are all sitting up for you."

It is a special honor in the Native American traditions to take someone on as a relative. It means that you will walk with them through life and hold that relationship as sacred. I did hear her say "grandson," and in my heart I had already accepted her as my Native Grandmother.

She continued on, saying, "They are all holding space for you to lift up. It's time for you to hold space for yourself. It's time for you to lift *you* up and be all you're meant to be."

Right there in that moment I sat up, and I knew something would be different.

Kevin and I went out to the fire and began to gather the last round of stones. He said to me, "I wasn't going to tell you, but it seems you need to know. When I put my hand on your back I had a vision. I had a vision of a white buffalo and a great bear. The white buffalo is you, and you are here to bring peace to everything. So it's time for you to own that. It is time for you to know that you are powerful beyond your imagination. I share this with you so that you can hold it and carry it forward with you."

I looked into the fire. Heck, I wanted to jump in the fire. I told him that I knew what I needed to do, I needed to cry, but I couldn't get it out.

He said, "All you have to do is let it go."

I looked deep in the fire. I could feel the fire burning on my skin. And all of a sudden, I started crying, and Kevin caught me as I dropped to my knees. Right there in that moment I was being birthed into that energy that started in New York. I was ready to explode through my heart and was ready to allow it to open up.

When we went back in the sweat lodge, one of the elders, Elly, said, "I have seen this before. This happens to all of those who are here to be prophets. You need to suck it up, this is what is meant to be for you."

We went back into the sweat lodge. I took a seat and sat up for this last round. I knew I had it in me, and everyone in there would help it awaken. At the very end of the sweat, as everyone was exiting, Grandmother said to me, "I'm proud of you, Grandson, you did great work. Now let us go and feast."

As we sat around and ate, I shared my experience in the sweat. We would all laugh at me. A story grew from the mouths of the elders, and you would have thought I was trying to dig my way to China. Funny how things grow, after the fact.

My new friend, Shelly, whom I met there, caught me in the moment and asked me if I wanted to do a vision quest. I had no clue what a vision quest was, so me being me, I said yes. She told me you have to sit out on the land with nothing, by yourself. I figured the Boy Scout in me would know how to eat off the land, so I should be good. She showed me around the land. I found my spot I would sit out, and another part to the journey would begin.

Grandmother Morningstar would always say to me, "Grandson, you don't have to walk on water, you know."

And I'd say to her, "Grandma, it is not just about actually walking on water. It is about creating the stillness inside that will allow me to walk on water. I want to be like the feather that floats so freely downstream towards the source that it never gets disrupted by the currents or the rocks. It gently lies on the body of water and flows downstream. If I can hold that space, then I can just float, and to me that is the greatest space that I can come into." And that's what I've been trying to do all my life: find a deep peace within myself that is absolutely unshakable.

Vision quest is a Native American ceremony, much like a right of passage. I started my first of four vision quests in 2007. On this first vision quest, I had the intention to see from my heart, to hear from my heart, and to speak from my heart. When you are on vision quest, you have a support person who comes to help the elder who is leading the quest. For my first quest, I asked my new friend, Hope, to support me along with Shelly.

Hope and I had developed a great relationship. We spent many nights together since the sweat lodge, and she helped me maintain my focus as I moved through the preparation of all that was to come on this quest. We had gotten to a point where we were figuring out just how we would continue our relationship. Just before I left for quest, her ex-boyfriend came back around. He was interesting in how he treated her, and I knew I was on a mission. So for me, I kept going and gave space for her to figure out just where she wanted her life to go. It was touch-and-go at one point, I wasn't sure if she was even going to join me for quest. She ended up coming the night before I left and said she was going because she did not want to desert me for something so important. I saw her spirit and knew that deep within was a person looking to dive into a new life. Yet, that was for her to determine.

We arrived on the land the night before I would go out. When we went out to set up my circle, I had two support people: my friend Hope and Grandmother. Shelly was awesome. She helped me figure out how to prepare my circle. She helped me to see just what needed to be cleared. To the west, there was a tree that had fallen. It was blocking the path of entryway. I had to clear this in order to have the energy come in, to allow all that needed to flow, and to enter into my circle. I also had to clear many other areas in order to make sure the space was set for the next three days.

While I was setting up the circle, Shelly asked if she was my girlfriend. I paused with a lot of hesitation, and said yes. She asked why I had not told Grandmother. My response was that she never really asked.

Once my circle was set, we went back to the house. I told Grandmother that my friend and I were in a relationship. She said, "Well, then, you all will share a room." During the night we talked about what our relationship was becoming. We discussed what would possibly be our future. We shared the night and closed our eyes.

The next day, I went to prepare to go out. As I sat looking

across the lake at my space, I noticed that everyone was chuckling. They were chuckling because they said they could see the spirits that were coming to spend the night with me. I laughed and said, "You guys are funny, you're just trying to mess with me."

All of a sudden this huge fog came blowing in, and Ciro said, "Can't you see them?"

I asked, "See who?"

He replied, "The people of the mist. Can't you see the beings coming?"

I looked, and to my amazement I saw legs walking underneath the fog. I've never seen anything like this, and here I was going out into the woods to spend three days by myself. Everyone laughed again, and now it was time to get prepared to go into the first sweat lodge.

Before we went into the sweat lodge, we were smudged and cleared with sage. I stood facing the fire with my friend nearby. Grandmother stood between us and said, "Grandson, look, look to the fire. Grandfather fire has come to see you."

As I gazed into the fire she said, "Look, you can see his shadow."

I looked above the fire, and there he was. A powerful presence, as if a being with blue, red, and silver armor had come out of the fire to awaken the warrior within me, to allow me to be the most powerful self that I could be in this lifetime. I knew this presence was more than just a being. I felt a kinship, a sense of connection I'd been looking for. I knew that the fire would take care of me for the rest of my journey.

During the sweat lodge I had many thoughts going through my head. I began to think about whether or not I could last without food or water for three days. I mean, my brother thought I was going to commit suicide and that would be the only reason I would go and try to do something like this. It was my calling. A time for me to move forward into my own healing process. After sitting in the sweat lodge, hearing all the many blessings and lessons from Grandmother, it was time for me to head across the lake and spend time alone.

We got a later start to the day than had originally been anticipated, so as soon as I got situated in my spot, the sun had begun to set. I must admit, I was pretty scared. I had no clue what would come out of the unknown, but I told myself: what will be, will be. I got in my sleeping bag, pulled it over my head, and dove in.

The next morning I was awakened by a woodpecker hammering away at this old tree. I could feel with each peck, my heart would begin to gain more power. On my first day alone, many animals came to visit. They shared their energy throughout my time out on the mountains. One of the most impactful moments came on the second day when I was resting. All of a sudden, I heard heavy footsteps running towards me. It sounded like it was going to stampede me as I lay on the ground. I sat up quickly and I looked. Coming from the south was a large buck. We made eye contact, and he stopped dead in his tracks. He stared at me, brushed his foot against the ground, bowed his head, and walked away. I knew he was telling me it was time to stop barreling over everyone in my life. It was time for me to move with ease and to care for others before caring for myself.

Later that same day, I started to feel hungry. I had these growing pains as a kid that would cause me to buckle over and not be able to move. I felt these pains coming on and knew that if it hit me, I would be in terrible pain. I remembered in the sweat lodge Grandmother saying, "If you need anything, just call on Spirit, and we will know to feed the fire. You will see smoke, and all will be taken care of. Now, I have a lot of faith in my prayers, yet this was something different. I new in this moment that I desperately needed my prayers answered in order to make it through the next day and night. So I put prayers out, asking to be fed. I looked across the lake and I saw smoke go up in the air, and to my astonishment, I was satisfied. I didn't need anything else. All I needed was to have a connection to Spirit, and Spirit would handle the rest.

Hours later, I was sitting and waiting, waiting for time to pass to do my walking meditation where I'd send my prayers up to all the directions so that when the quest was finished, everything would be known. Suddenly, I looked up, and diving in the lake was a huge bald eagle. The eagle dove into the water once as it moved from the east, then again as it moved from the west. Then it came from the north, and finally as it came back around from the south, it pulled a huge bass out of the water, flew up and sat in a tree, and began to eat. The eagle sat in the tree and ate for several hours. It would look at me, and it was like it was feeding me. I felt my soul begin to ignite and the strength within me lift up. I knew I was going to be okay. Once the remarkable bird was finished, it left and flew off towards the north. For me, this eagle had represented that it was time for me to move forward with my own visions. It was time for me to stay the course and continue on with my own healing. It was time for me to begin to understand my highest self. Just speak, see, hear, and feel from my heart. I knew this eagle had left me a huge gift.

As the day turned into night, I was reminded that I was told that if I was happy, to howl like the wolf. I felt great, even though I'd been attacked by mosquitoes the night before. I was ecstatic about all that was possible to come forward in my life. I even thought about my friend across the lake, that I was yearning to have a companion to walk this journey. As the sun began to set, I started to howl. As I continued, everything seemed to get quiet. I was later told that they could hear me across the lake, and at first they all laughed, and then they realized that the pack of coyotes that was led by wolf were running by. Grandmother had said to them, "I don't think my grandson knows what he's doing right now."

By the time the sun had set and everything began to get dark, the coyotes had made their way around the lake. They created a circle around me, and all I could see were green eyes. For some reason, I never got nervous. I knew that they were there to awaken something within me, and all would be okay once again. I knew that I just received coyote medicine, and that I would be able to stand now in moments that needed to be serious, playful, and noisy as well. The coyotes had blessed me with a new energy, and energy to be okay what's in any and every moment.

During the night I was paid a visit from one of creations on the mountain. This time I was visited by a mother bear and her three cubs. The mother bear set back in the trees and watched over as the three cubs came down to my circle. The cubs ran around in circles and just continued to move around me, as I observed. They were playing, and I could feel their energy of joy and innocence. I felt the energy rising once again. I can see how the mother was protective and standing just to observe, like watching your children at the park. I felt and received a beautiful shift from these bears, of my body, mind, and spirit. This would later serve me for many years to come

On my last night of this first vision quest, I was preparing myself to handle the mosquitoes that had bit me up the previous night. I went deep into my sleeping bag, but the top of my head was still sticking out. Once again, I would endure the attacks. Midway through the night, I heard something. I heard something land, and I heard feet jump onto the ground. Something was walking over to me, yet I was too scared to look. I was worried that whatever was coming, I wasn't sure I was ready to see it. I lay there in terror, listening to it come closer and closer, until the footsteps stopped right at my head. I felt something grab my sleeping bag and lift it up. I had no clue who could be out there with me. I closed my eyes tighter, too afraid to want to acknowledge what was before me. I felt a hand touch my head. It pushed on me and said, "Get deeper, Grandson."

There was suddenly more space in my sleeping bag. I was able to get in deeper and knew everything was okay. My heart rate began to slow down, and I started to breathe easier, knowing I would always be looked after. Then all of a sudden, I heard the galloping of a horse and what sounded like it leaping off of a nearby rock. Then there was silence, as if when it leaped, it flew off into the heavens. I then opened my eyes and peeked out of the sleeping bag and yelled like a child, "Grandmother, Grandmother! It's your horse!" I then paused and realized how strange I sounded, even to myself. It was a very interesting night.

I woke up the next morning, and on the face of a rock nearby me was a picture that I copied into my journal. In the image there was a fire, representing what I always knew would burn inside me. There was the moon and the sun that symbolized that I would live for many mornings and nights. There was a circle in the middle that seemed to form the shape of a peace sign that I knew was deeply planted in my heart. Then there was my heart at the top, with two hawks above it, representing healing. This symbol will forever be worn inside of me for all of my days.

After a couple hours, I looked up and saw Hope was coming across the lake in a canoe to pick me up. She was being brought by Roberto, and I was going to have to gather my stuff and head back in. I felt amazing, I felt invigorated, and ready for anything. As I began to make eye contact with my friend, I heard spirits say let her go. My mind was silent, and I knew deep in my heart this was spoken from truth.

When she arrived, she helped as I packed my things. She looked awesome, she had a glow of excitement and joy. She shared with me that she was worried about all the animals and me sitting out in the mountains alone. It was nice to see her excitement in seeing I was safe. After packing my stuff and putting it in the canoe, she helped me leave nuts and berries behind for the animals, thanking them for allowing me to disrupt their home. Once we started back, she handed me a flask of water. I thought I still wasn't going to be allowed to have any water, so I was so excited about this little bit. The water tasted like gold, it was absolutely the best water I have ever had. Really never again, have I tasted something so pure. My friend began to explain how she had written me a letter explaining exactly how she felt that we would be going forward. She was so excited, that she didn't even give me time to get back to read the letter. She told me how she saw us spending the rest of our lives together, that she was ready to commit to a deeper relationship, to a deeper understanding of just where we would go on our journey. Once we had the closing feast, we loaded up the car and headed home.

One of the major lessons I picked up on my first vision quest was how we had to first look inside ourselves, in order to heal those around us. I took the time to go and heal the breaks in my heart to become complete from the inside out. On the way home, we decided to stop at my favorite rest stop. It's a location at the top of the mountain, where there is a Starbucks and many other restaurants. We stopped and got ice cream and began to walk through the shops. I can remember my friend reached out to hold my hand and for some reason I felt hesitant. I would just let it go, as I know myself, and I often just like space.

Over the next couple days, I was told to stay out of crowds and give myself space to recover from sitting out in the mountains. My first meditation at home, I noticed something different. What was different was when I began to breathe, I could feel how I was shifting. I had a strange sensation when I was breathing. I began to feel my breath coming out on top of my nose, as opposed to coming out of my nostrils pointing down. I could feel my face shifting into what felt like a beak. I began to wonder if this was truly happening. As soon as I reached to feel my face, it all stopped. So many things seemed to be coming forward for me, and only time would tell what would come next and when.

A friend of mine connected with me and said she would drive me around to the grocery store and to run errands, but first, she wanted to stop for her annual tarot reading. I said I was fine with going along. I've never had one, so I figured it could be interesting to see what it was like. When we walked in, she asked the lady if it was okay for me to watch.

Once we entered the room, she said, "I cannot give you a reading; his vibration is too high. So high that if I try and give you a reading, I would actually only be reading his energy. It seems that he has been doing some work in the mountains, and so I'll have to read for you alone." I stepped out and as I looked back, I saw a look of concern on the lady's face.

My friend had her reading, and afterwards the lady asked if she could talk to me. She said that I had someone trying to send black magic my way, and if I was open to it, she would like to help me for free. At this point, I'd been through a lot, so when someone wanted to help me with no strings attached, I figured I better allow it. She had many things with Jesus, hanging and placed around her establishment, and with my Catholic upbringing and all, I figured she may know something.

We ended up scheduling appointments for the next six weeks. She would inform me of people that I needed to watch out for and protect me from the things that were being done behind my back. Having the seer watching over me seemed to work well, and aligned with what I knew having grown up near the Bayou in Louisiana. So we would continue to work together for the next year.

A few days had passed since I'd seen Hope. The next time I spoke to Grandmother she would ask me how things were going in my relationship with her. I told her pretty good and that I actually hadn't seen her in a couple days. "We were supposed to have dinner tonight," I said. She responded with, "So you didn't listen to spirit! They said get rid of her." I paused for a moment to reflect on what she just said. "Did you hear me?" she asked. "They said get rid of her."

"Okay," I said.

"No, you're not listening. They said get rid of her," she insisted.

I said, "Okay, I hear you. I will get rid of her tonight."

She responded, "Alright, let me know how it goes."

Later that evening, we were getting together to go to dinner. When we met, she said she wanted to talk. It was interesting how things lined up. She had seen her ex-boyfriend since we got back, and she wanted to have space. It's funny how things worked out and just naturally moved forward after sitting in the mountains. Being in my first week from coming off the mountain, I noticed that the deep lines of pain lingering from my life were being carried into my current situation. It was going to take some time to allow it to pass. A few days passed, and I had some time alone. I was told for the next week to create space, stay out of crowds, and continue to watch me, especially my dreams.

The next morning, I called Grandmother to let her know the outcome of our dinner. "How do you feel?" she said.

I replied, "I'm okay. Seems like it's what should be."

She continued, "Okay, now I want you to go and write down everything you could possibly want in a partner. I know that you enjoy women, so once you have completed this list, I want you to go out with as many women as you want, and while you do that, I want you to pay attention to your list. If there is anything that does not fit from your list with the person you're with, shift it in you, and it will shift in those you are with as well."

And that's exactly what I did. I chose to go and just have fun. I really had no strings attached. I was looking for someone to come into my life, and it would happen when the time was right.

Life seemed to move really fast. In the next three months there seemed to be a lot going on. I was moving into a second divorce and was going to need to move out of my house sooner than later. I was just getting myself situated in this new vibration. One day after I taught a class, I was sitting at the computer doing some work. One of teachers, Maria Fratus, was sitting next to me. All of a sudden she said something that was very strange. "Oh my God," she said, "here comes your future wife."

I looked at her and said, "That is one of the dumbest things I think you've ever said." I looked up and said, "Oh crap." For some reason, I, too, thought: there is someone that is going to be in my life.

In walked Lindsay, and before ever even taking a class, she wanted to sign up for an annual membership. Now, if things weren't strange enough, I knew something was going to have to be different. When she finally came to class, I began to sense that something was there. After class, I went and talked to her and said, "I really would rather not date students, so before you become a student, I would like to ask you out."

She replied, "Well, that's strange. I just broke up with my boyfriend yesterday, and it may be a bit too soon. I think I need to have some time alone before I start dating."

I said, "Well, I figured I'd say what I needed to say, and either it will come to be or it won't."

Some time had passed, and I figured I'd give it one more shot. I asked her again, and she hesitated. The response in my head to this was to move on, so then I presented her with, "You were a college lacrosse player, and I've asked, and I'm not going to ask again. I'm passing you the ball, and so you decide if there's anything that'll come of this."

As soon as I said that she responded with, "What are you doing now?"

I was thrown off, and then I replied, "Nothing." We ended up going to get a cup of tea and then made plans to go get dinner the next night.

We went out to dinner and had a great time. I shared about vision quest and all the things that came of that. She was pretty open in her listening and accepting in all that I was sharing, even though later I learned that she thought it was pretty crazy to hear me say that I was outside without food or water for three days. She never heard of anything like it.

From that moment on, we became closer and closer. I was scheduled to move into my new house that was numbered 42. The number 42 has great significance, as it is a universal number for creation. This home would play out many powerful moments in my life for years to come.

Lindsay happened to have the next day off and offered to come by to help me move into the new place. I was astounded and thrilled by her kind gesture. We ended up hanging out for several days to come. And there you have it: I knew my life once again was about to shift and move in a really fast way. I was moving out of one life and moving into another. I truly enjoyed watching her operate from moment to moment. I would grow to understand more about myself in the reflection of her.

As time moved on, I was getting closer to my next vision quest. It seemed only appropriate, with the support she gave me during the recent transitions in my life, that she would become my support person and my partner through the next several years of my life.

After my first vision quest, I was so used to sitting outside I continued to head to the reservoir in order to continue to feel the power of my connection to nature. One day while I was there, I had two bald eagles fly overhead. I then got a message from Lindsay saying she forgot something at home and could I bring it to her. As I arrived at the hospital where she worked, there were the two eagles flying overhead. Then I went downtown, and there they were again. I knew they were going to be with me for the rest of my life; the eagle nation would come to my aid whenever needed.

After teaching a class one day, one of my students came to me and asked if I had ever been to a vipassana retreat. "No, I haven't," I said.

Her response was, "I think you would enjoy it."

I took a look at their website. I thought a couple of days in silence and meditation sounded great, so I applied. I was floored when I heard back immediately, and what I failed to realize was, it was not just a weekend, rather ten days in silence. I would have a month to prepare. Having sat in the mountains for three days, I figured I could handle it. I spent extra time meditating and gathering several items: a block, meditation cushion, mala beads, and a floor chair back. I packed my clothes and I was ready. I asked Lindsay to take me to the center, figuring if I was dropped off, I would have no choice but to stay. This was my mode of operation from day one in this life. I commit to doing something, I go all in, and get it done.

Upon arrival, I checked in and realized I was going to have to carry all of my stuff back and forth to the housing unit, so I asked Lindsay to take everything back home. I kept my clothes, my toiletries, and a block to meditate on. For the next ten days, I would have the opportunity to stop and look into myself. We were instructed to release all of our old practices, no books, no writing, no talking, and no eye contact. There were three guys that decided to take their college spring break and do ten days in silence. They chose to be there, instead of off partying, and that in itself was really special in my eyes.

For whatever reason, people tend to gravitate towards me, and these guys were no different. I think it has to do with the initial space I hold, as I tend to sit back and observe, then I plug into my surroundings and go after it. These guys had snuck paper into the dorm and asked if I wanted a couple of three-inch squares. I figured this would give me just enough to write two or three words to be able to remember what came up for me in key moments during my time there.

It seemed as though I experienced the transformation in what seemed like four sections. This seems to coincide with how everything unfolds in the Native American ceremonies, as well. Four represents the cycles of the year, the four directions, and four phases of life. So it appeared that there were many reasons and connections for me to take the time to sit in silence for ten days. The cycles for me were first landing with a solid foundation, then a willingness to stay the course, then understanding what I am bringing forward in my life in the name of my spiritual connection, and finally, live it in every way.

The first cycle started on day one and continued for two more days. We were taught techniques to bring forward our meditation practice. The first part was to get present to our breath. Although we were breathing yesterday and likely will be breathing tomorrow, the focus was to breathe right here and now. We are in our breath every day, and every moment. It is our breath that can teach us a lot about how we can operate.

Take a moment and breathe in and hold your breath. Wait as long as you can. Now breathe out and hold your breath. Hold it as long as you can. What you will notice is if you take in as much as you can, you eventually have to give air out. You will also become aware of the fact that if you give as much as you can you will eventually have to receive air at some point. So the foundation of my breath, for me, was a great teacher to begin to shape the rest of my time in silence. I had to realize that in every moment I could reflect on the principle teaching of my breath. I can live in balance and learn to be appropriate as to when I give and when I am open to receiving the gift of the moment. There were several other techniques that landed for me that I've added to my daily meditation practice from this experience alone.

As we moved through the first three days, I began to feel a disconnect from my everyday life. I went through the point where I missed being home with Lindsay. I missed my kids, although I had grown accustomed to seeing them on and off. I also found that I began to feel a panic about the studio, whether the team would maintain it in my absence. At one point, I seriously considered leaving. I came to my senses when I realized it was twenty-five miles from even having access to a phone. I made the choice to be dropped off. I was going to have to suck it up.

The next night our teacher Satya Narayan Goenka, aka "S. N. Goenka," would speak. He told us, "Tomorrow, you will likely want to quit."

I thought to myself, *You are a day late. I just spent the last twelve hours plotting my escape.* This is when it got a little fun, and I realized my brain was pulling in the information a day ahead of what was being taught. I began to connect the dots that there was something deeper at work. This felt as if I had already been in these teachings of master Buddha. Cycle two was complete, and I had committed to staying the course.

The next cycle for me seemed to play out over several days. I was faced with a repetitive thought. Even though Lindsay had said at one point she did not want to teach, I kept thinking maybe it was something that would fit. In my opinion, she would be a natural. We lived together, so meeting to coach and develop wouldn't be an issue, and she already knew the sequence from practicing. She would never need to go through a formal training, because what could be better than diving into the life together?

The next morning, I realized that I wanted to do whatever it took to reach the deepest part of my own understanding. I wanted to dive in and uncover all that was there for me to see that had yet to be seen. I headed over to eat breakfast and realized that for me to start, I would let go of one of my most precious rituals. I have been praying over my food for as long as I can remember. When I first started praying, I used to pray the traditional Catholic prayer to bless my food. Then as time passed, something clicked within and I began to allow my prayers to flow from my heart. I would end each prayer saying, "May this strengthen my heart, bless my soul, and nourish my body." Now, I sat there, letting go of something I used to flow everything in my life. I have used my prayers to move beyond many obstacles. After breakfast and on my way to morning meditation, I felt the vibration building in my heart. I looked up and like clockwork, above me about twenty feet, were two hawks, and out sixty feet above, were two eagles. I looked towards the sky and in my heart asked them all to leave. I asked them to leave, so that I may know just what I was to do.

Days passed, and I began to feel off. I was staying in a room with fifteen guys. The chorus of snores would leave me restless. At this point, I realized that in order to get some type of sleep, I would have to rush back before everyone, hustle and brush my teeth, and try to fall asleep before everyone else went to bed. It was as if they knew at 2:00 a.m. I was going to be rested enough to wake up. I would stay in bed as long as I could. Because I had nothing else to do, I would get up and brush my teeth. Sometimes I would brush my teeth three or four times during the night.

On day eight, I began to feel like I was lost. I loved my connection to nature, I knew there was more to life, and being connected to all was an important piece to who I was and what I loved about living. I went to breakfast, then to morning meditation; all seemed to be flowing as it had been. After lunch, I went back to the room to rest. The three college guys cornered me in the room.

"We need to talk," they said, "We know you are in noble science, but you are the only person here we know could handle this. You know the man with the panda teddy bear?" I nodded. "Every time we are left alone, he corners us and gets naked. He runs around the room and acts like a panda bear."

Now, inside, I was like, "No way!" They took me into the room where he was, and sure enough, there he was exactly as they had described, rolling around, feet up in the air on a tree trunk that was in the middle of the room. This was strange to me, and the three guys were more than taken back. We all left the scene and went our separate ways.

I sat outside and looked over to my left. There, on top of a stump, was a twelve foot brown snake. This was yet another reminder for me of the oneness that I feel with nature, of my Native American traditions, and connection to Spirit that would continue to open me up. The snake energy is that of radical transformation.

I went to visit with our group leader. We were allowed to go and speak if and when we had any major concerns. I broke silence to explain what was transpiring. The leader had a tough time holding back his laughter. We looked out the window, and there we saw the man outside boxing. They ended up bringing him in and explaining how his actions were inappropriate. I was slightly alarmed that they allowed him to stay at first, but he promised to settle down, and all was clear from then on.

After a meditation that afternoon, I had a deep sadness that came forward. I knew that I was looking for my hawks and eagles to return. I was aware that my connection to them was something I wanted from deep within me. My spirit connects to my rituals and I have faith in them. My spiritual ways are my foundation, and I trust in them. I came outside after our meditation, and paused. I took a moment to call on the hawks and eagles. I knew I wanted them to return. Deep in my heart, I knew they were a part of me. I looked to the sky, and others walking by began to look up to see what I was looking for. I went and sat on a picnic table nearby and called again for the hawks to come. I called again for the eagles to appear. About thirty minutes into our break, the hawks returned, then the eagles. I was beyond happy to have them back, to know that I would always have their support no matter where I went from this day forward. I would go back in to meditate, and pure joy fell upon me. I knew I was in a new place, transformed with a renewed faith in and of myself. I went to dinner that night, and I would choose to pray before my meal, to call it all in, and live from the power of what is part of the life I chose. I understand that everything is impermanent, and yet I know I am connected to all and am okay being in the bliss of all that is, was, and will be.

There were moments where my mind still wanted to play the game. Moments my mind began to make jokes about everything. Jokes that made no sense. In these moments, I knew my mind only wanted to survive. It wanted me to continue to pay attention to the limitations. Yet I knew on the other side of every joke was freedom, and if I let go of all attachments, I would truly find a new place to live from, a place of pure joy. I began to connect even deeper; I began to understand that the pains in my body were there to teach me. This was now new space and new connection to a deeper understanding of it all.

As the sun began to set, I went through my nightly rituals. I rushed to the room, looking to fall asleep before everyone else had gone down. This night something seemed different, something was moving in the air. I fell asleep early, and this time when I woke, there was pure silence amongst the room. I was just about to get out of bed when I heard a voice say, "Not tonight, stay where you are." I paused, and then sat up in my bed. I began to hear voices. One voice was coming from deep within myself, and there were other voices, asking questions. All of the sudden, one of the college kids from the bunk next to me leaned over and said, "How long did you say you've been here?"

I looked at him and I responded, "Thirty-three thousand years. I have been here thirty-three thousand years."

The number thirty-three refers to the Trinity and means that you are receiving divine protection, help, and guidance. In most cases, if you are seeing a lot of 3s, for those that follow Angel Number Signs, this means you have a close connection to Jesus, God the Son, in the Holy Trinity. Thirty-three means that Jesus is with you, helping, and guiding you. I knew all was taken care. There was nothing left to think about, everything was in divine order.

As we entered into the last day, I felt prepared and wanted to finish strong. I was dialed in, and ready to experience all that was to come. I was open to the fact that, today, we would endure a two-hour meditation. The first hour was guided. For the second hour, we would look to land in complete stillness and observe what was coming to be. I saw how everything was transforming. I experienced how scanning my body was much like a clearing of all energy blocks, and after this hour, I would land in a new way all together. I felt how I was in my power, and when I felt off, I would remember this was not just for me. This was for anyone who may be looking for me to provide anything to help them move forward as well. After this meditation, we would break silence and begin to integrate back into connecting with other people.

I had an opportunity to visit with others who were in the meditation experience with me. I learned that my peers saw me as a pillar, or a light, helping them be strong through it all. They shared how they sensed I was strong and ready to help anyone that needed it. What amazed me is I hadn't met anyone or had a chance to speak to anyone, outside of hearing the college guys explain the panda experience. We all got a great laugh out of that conversation; even Mr. Panda himself was able to laugh at himself.

One of the volunteers came over to have a conversation after we went to eat. He asked me how my experience was. I let him know how it seemed pretty tough, yet something was pulling me forward. He would go on to explain how his friend was a great musician that once came to the meditation. He would leave the meditation with a message to return to the aboriginal people of Australia and discover his roots. When he returned he was greeted by the people and the elder that led them. She told him they had sent him away to send his message out and discover his way home. As the story goes, they always look for one person in the training they know they can pull through that will create a major shift on the planet. He looked me in the eyes and said, "This time, from the moment you walked in, we all knew you were the one. As you would come through this, you would be the greatest impact the world had seen." I was humbled and honored by this, and I was still uncertain on where that would take me next.

I was excited to leave and really had no clue what was in store. I was open to anything and just happy to go home. Lindsay came to pick me up, and she told about the two eagles that were sitting in the field. She said that she had to stop the car because she saw two huge birds in the field and wanted to know what they were. When she got out of the car, she realized they were bald eagles. On the way home, as we turned out of the driveway of the center, there they were again. The two bald eagles flew overhead and traveled with us for quite some time on the drive home.

Lindsay kept looking at me and saying, "Something seems so different."

I responded, "I'm not sure. I am just here, the same me."

As she went to get out of the car to get gas, she paused and said, "Smile for me."

I smiled and she said, "Oh my god. It is your teeth: why are they soooo white?"

"Well," I said, "I couldn't sleep, so my pastime was to brush my teeth, like to pass the time." She laughed, we got gas, and headed home.

Once we got home, Lindsay would have to prepare to go to work. "Will you be okay?" she asked. As I lay in our bed, I said, "Yes, I am going to just rest up."

She replied, "Okay, well I wrote you every day. It is all in the journal next to you on the nightstand."

I responded, "Really? Every day?"

"Yes, every day," she said. "I shared how I wrote a subject each day on a piece of paper, and how and why it was all I was able to do."

The windows were open in our bedroom and all of a sudden, I stopped and started looking around frantically. "Sid," she said, "what is wrong?"

I quickly asked, "What is that noise?"

"What noise Sid?" she replied.

I proceeded, "There. Do you hear it?"

"You mean the siren?" she asked.

"What?" I said, "Ohhhhh yeah, I haven't heard that." She again asked if I would be okay. I responded, "Yes, I am good. I will read what you wrote." As I began to read, I realized she had written about every subject I had written on my little piece of paper. She wrote about each subject I noted, on the exact same days. On day five, she wrote about teaching. She wrote about it all with great clarity. It is amazing how connected we all can be when we get out of the way. It was meant to be that we would walk this journey together over the next several years.

Everything seemed to be moving with a great deal of velocity. It was time for my next vision quest. I knew there was more to come. I saw that, after my first quest, so much of my life had been shifted. As I prepared for my second vision quest, I wanted to truly realize God. I wanted to see God clearly from perspectives that I didn't quite understand.

I had been gifted a pet wolf from Lindsay and the community. I chose to name her "Shiva." She would become one of my greatest teachers for the next seven years. When I would sit and offer up prayers during my preparation for the quest, she would lie down and watch. She would get so still in these moments. Now, understand, as a young cub, she would sense how my energy was so antsy, as I am always on the move, and she would eat all the blinds in the house. She would always come into the energy of those around her. When we first got her we had to spend time helping her trust being comfortable in her new pack. We'd take naps with her on the floor to help her transition. I had to learn to lead as the alpha, even when I wanted to be lazy. Shiva was truly an amazing soul.

A couple months before I would head out on my second vision quest, I took a group of people up to the land for a retreat. We would spend time doing various activities. We would have yoga classes in the lodge, often participate in sweat lodges, spend time sitting in meditation on the mountain, and would have the opportunity to enjoy visiting with my grandmother. This particular visit, my grandmother said that she thought I needed a break. She said that I did look tired, and we had been working hard. She suggested that we take the night off and go see a movie. I suggested we do a yoga practice, eat dinner, and then head to the movie.

That's exactly how the day would unfold. It was interesting at the end of our yoga practice, as the sun began to set, we ended in savasana and I began to notice the energy in the room. I lay there and felt how I was being scanned. I could feel the energy flowing up and down, from my head to my toes, and then from my toes to my head. This happened several times, and I knew something had just shifted. I lay still for a while and then we got up to go have dinner. I sat and talked with Grandmother during dinner, and she told me the movie I should go see was called *Crystal Skulls*.

She said, "You need to pay attention to a specific part. I'm not going to tell you what it is, but you will know."

We went to the movie and Grandmother was right, I was tired. I fell asleep within the first five minutes of the movie, only to wake up right when they made their way to the cave where they found all the crystal skulls. As the skulls came together, they would link in energy. These skulls were then connected and would hold the energy of the earth. I then fell back asleep.

When we returned, Grandmother asked me how the movie was. I responded, "I really don't know, I fell asleep for most of it. Yet I woke up right when they found these crystal skulls, and when they put them together, it seemed like there was a connection to the skulls and the essence of everything."

She laughed and said, "That's exactly what you needed to see."

The next day we headed home. I would continue to prepare for the quest and get ready to come back and sit in the mountains. I would take time to pray every night.

At this point, TD had come to live with us; it was great having both of my boys living with me. We went out to have dinner, and upon returning, I saw something in the sky. The boys had already dashed out of the car and were heading into the house. I looked up and said to Lindsay, "Look up." She saw it, too. I called for the boys to come back out and for them to quickly look up. There it was, as clear as the night sky, a saucer hovering over top of us.

Sid IV, who is often reactive, said, "What the heck is that? What do you think it is?" He knew exactly what it was. He continued, "Why do you do this to me? All I want to do is go to college and play football. I don't want to know of these things. I want to live life and just be okay with life as it is."

I looked at TD, and we smiled at each other, as we typically do in moments like these. The differences I witness in my boys make me smile. TD would take things in stride as they are, and Sid IV would want things to be the way he wanted them to be. Once again, I would see just what I am meant to see.

I returned to the mountains. I was fully prepared to sit out and go in. Go in again and see just what was out there that I was looking to understand. This time, there were objects that appeared in the sky that were unidentifiable. I saw them and would often think that they were communicating to me. There were voices that I'd hear, speaking to me from many different directions. I remember on the second night, the voices came as I was lying down to rest. "Hey, hey," she said, "He is over here. Come on, come on." I thought to myself, "Whoa, who are they looking for? Are they talking about me?"

I closed my eyes, as I wasn't sure I was ready to truly see who they were. I felt their energy surround me in the moment, and I heard a female voice say, "I will take his head." A deep male's voice said, "I'll take his feet." A higher female voice said, "I have this side," and another said, "I have this side." I could not move. I was pinned down, and again I felt this energy flow over my body. I felt the scanning of my body and an awakening of every cell. I knew I was being shifted to vibrate at a higher frequency.

The next day, I was done. I was out of my body for twenty-four hours. I was paralyzed with the exception of going to the bathroom one time. When I did, I literally could not have been ten feet from my circle, yet, I could not find my way back. When I finally did get back, I sat on the ground and asked: is it done? My body shook from side to side, telling me no. I had tuned into a frequency of truth from within, the truth of a knowing, that a yes is a yes, and a no is a no, and it is known on a cellular level.

I would spend the next day going deeper, feeling surges of energy come through. On the third night, my friend the bald eagle would come visit once again, perching himself in a tree nearby. This time he sat to the northwest, as if to direct me, to make sure I would see what was going to transpire next. I heard from within, "Just watch." I looked, and as the sun started to set, it was revealed. I saw a cave. The crystal cave was shown. There it was, and it all made sense to me. Grandmother and I would discuss this in the days to come, and I would further understand the connection to everything. There was a trust factor that I had to come into this time around, in order to have faith in something greater than myself. I learned on this vision quest that I would be complete as long as I was complete in my heart.

We finished the quest with a sweat lodge, and then enjoyed a feast. On previous retreats or quests, I would leave the land once they came to an end. This time, we decided to stay another night in the lodge. That night, we went up to the open grass, lay down, and looked at the stars. Grandmother began to talk about my quest, and would say, "Look up, Grandson, see out there, see everything. You are everything. If you want to realize yourself, you must see everything."

At this point, the other people there were in conversation. Being that I just spent four days alone in silence, I wanted to feel the peace of that continue. I nudged Lindsay and suggested we go down to the dock. Sitting on the dock, we continued to look up into the stars. I noticed I would be called to look at a star. That star would begin to flash, and then it would move. After watching this happen several times, I invited Lindsay to look and observe the next one that would to call me. "Do you see it?" I would ask, "Watch it flash, and then watch it move." We stayed there for at least an hour and counted fourteen times that we would witness the phenomenon that we could only describe as flying saucers, as they were clearly nothing like what you would describe as shooting stars.

Now you may say it was a figment of my imagination, but what I know is that army trucks and helicopters eventually came to the land. For some reason we have this belief to defend ourselves over something that may not be able to even be defended. I mean, these ships are so much larger than what we have, I'm not sure we have the ability to defend anything. I mean, I guess you take enough ants and cover a human with them, the ants could take over. So maybe that is the concept of the military that showed up. Later we went on to discover that you could now google the address of the land and find your way there. Before this night, you couldn't find Turtle Acres on Google maps.

Just before leaving, I told my grandmother that I felt exhausted and may need a break for a year from questing. She said she understood, and that maybe I should just let it be. I knew I had landed in a space much deeper and would want to sit, settle, and be in it. I gave her a hug and said I would talk to her soon.

As soon as I made it to the end of the driveway, I got a call from my mom. This time around, my family was different. There was no real fear for them, as I had made it through the first one and I came out alive. "Hi there, Son," my mom said, as she usually does when she calls. "How was it?"

"It was great. Lots came through and I feel great." I replied.

"Well, we wanted to check in and see how it went. We also wanted to let you know that if you go out again, we are coming to support you."

I paused for a moment and said, "Well, then, I will see you out here next year." I hung up the phone and called my grandmother to share the miracle that had just occurred and that I felt a need to bring this forward for them.

CORNERSTONE FOUR
Stay Open to the Practice

To *be*, is simple. Sit with all that is and stay present to what is at hand. In order to be, allow things to be as they are, nothing added, and nothing subtracted. Sit and realize that all that is in front of you is present. It is in the present moment that all is clear and exactly as it needs to be. It is easy for us to move through moments looking to control what is taking place, to resist and forget how to engage in the flow. This is an opportunity to allow grace to come in, free of any mind chatter of resistance. As we operate in this human existence, and we enter into the fourth cornerstone, we will flow between the fourth, third, and second cornerstone. As a person moves through each cornerstone, they learn to operate from a place of connection to the infinite.

Meditation helps everyone to understand how to be, to understand how from a sense of being, we have access to all that was, is, and will be. *We use alcohol to take the edge off; now that you're in your meditation practice, you'll find the edges are off when you're balanced.* Your meditation practice will bring you into balance. My meditation practice came along well before my *asana* practice. I was fortunate to have coaches from eight years of age on, to help me to see the benefits of a quiet and focused mind. Having sat still since my formative years, getting open to the freedom in my mind, has given me access to creativity, poise, the ability to remain calm under pressure, faith, and ultimately, love for life and all forms. I recall during my ten days in silence, I discovered that I gained access just by seeing my life and allowing it to unfold in the direction I desired. It is in the mental game that my greatest advancements have begun.

An elite human being is free to find that they are able to reach for their best in every moment. When we find space from controlling the outcome, we are able to dive into the flow of all and create a deeper space of being with Spirit. Our way to the total freedom is by diving into the space of our minds. When we begin to work in the Mind Field Meditation System, we are able to create a new operating system that will create the results of the greatest destiny. Mind Field Meditation System gives us access to the space missed by many. In the mind field, we can discover our greatest connection to creativity. As we first begin to work in the Mind Field Meditation System, we want to establish one point and focus of our thoughts. You will find through the foundation of your meditation practice that you will fine-tune a connection to your body as an instrument, guiding you to the deeper understanding in connection to your highest self.

The stage was set. With my third vision quest, I went out for my family. It was here in the process of my third vision quest I would begin to move into the final cornerstone, and I would simply be peace for all. I knew I wanted to make sure that everything would be healed in order for me to continue to build a life of peace. Through this year of preparation, I would sit back and observe just where there was a place for me to see how I could learn to breathe new energy into moments that were sitting in a lack of peace.

By the time I had gotten to the quest, I had reached a place of full acceptance. I had sat in a place of witnessing all who were around me. I had now seen how everyone was viewing things from their perspectives. I recall early on, when I was in one of my first relationships, how my mom sat me down and said, "Not everyone thinks like you." So the same can be said for anyone else. I will likely not think the way anyone else does either. It is okay to allow someone else to have their own experience. I began to see the simple things in life and how the human side of me has chosen to see things from a harder place. I can allow myself space to let go of being tangled in the webs that everyone weaves.

Imagine if you go to the local coffee shop, and when you look at the menu, you see they have tea. You choose to order a tea. If they bring you a tea because that is what you wanted, you will likely be content and drink your tea. Now, if instead of your tea they bring you a mocha coffee, you can choose to leave it, and ask for your tea. I began to realize that too often, someone is offering me a cup of coffee, and I want tea, but I'd drink the coffee anyway. It really is that simple. I have chosen not to drink someone else's drink, even if they choose to serve it to me. It is up to all of us to be like the spider and weave the world we want to see in front of us, inside and out.

On my way to my third quest, I began to see how my reflection was looking different than I desired. I thought my family wasn't going to be able to make it. It was amazing to me, how my reflection was coming out and showing just where I wavered in my commitment to finish. I knew no matter what, I was going out for my family. I knew that they would feel it no matter what. I knew that as long as I continued to shift *me*, I would impact my family.

We continued through the normal rituals in preparation to going out. This time I was going out, knowing my work was done. I felt a deep unshakable peace within. I knew all was happening in divine order. I went out, and everything about my time out was a deep state of peace. I had a vision of a pipe, which I now carry, and of me standing on the shoulders of the seven generations before me. I knew that all was coming through. I would later find out that my friend Shelly, one of my support people, also saw a vision of a peace pipe in the fire as I sat out, and knew it was to be. I felt peace in every way, and at one point I heard a bear roar at a person who was out on the other side of the mountain, and I was still at peace. I thought of my parents and knew I had a deep peace with them, as well. I was unaware that across the lake, my parents had arrived. As nightfall came, they would begin their journey. Later I was told how both of my parents were worried about my safety. They stayed up in the middle of the night, praying and holding space for all to be easy for me. Little did they know, I had already moved through the tougher moments.

When I came in on the final morning, to my surprise, there they were. I can remember the smile on my face, and the joy in my heart. The pure love I felt for both of my parents was a beautiful thing. After every quest, I would sit with my grandmother, and talk about what came to me. I shared how at one point, I grabbed my pen and journal and began to write. I wrote page after page, after page, after page. It was as if my hand just couldn't stop, giving way to a stream of consciousness that would provide an explanation of what it is to be connected and at ease with all that is.

Grandmother explained that what I had was the wisdom of the pleiadian grandmothers—the same thirteen grandmothers who would represent those mothers of the crystal skulls. In this moment, she began to pause and start listening. From that moment, I connected with my grandmother. I knew there was a higher calling. I witnessed how my life had flipped upside down. I had seen how I had transformed, and here I am. I know that I am on a mission.

Just then grandmother began to explain that Spirit had a question to ask. "Would you like to hear?" she said.

"Yes, I am ready to hear," I replied.

She continued, "Now know that what I am about to share comes with a great deal of responsibility. Should you choose to not take this on, it is okay."

"Thank you." I said.

"The world is waiting for someone to carry the torch and bring peace forward. Know that taking on this mission, will continue to transform your world," she said.

"I understand," I said.

She asked, "Will you take on this mission?"

I looked her in the eyes and said, "Yes, I accept it."

"Spirit has a name for you," she said. We walked over to the fire, and she began to pray. "Here before you stands your son, 'He Brings Peace,'" she exclaimed. She began to cleanse me with sage, starting at my feet. "May he walk the earth knowing you will always support him, may you clear everything behind him, may you bless all that is before him, may you keep his heart open and lift him up, and may you keep everything above him clear."

We hugged, and in this moment, I knew all was good.

At this point, I still was not talking yet, nor having physical contact with anyone, outside of sharing one-on-one with my grandmother. It is tradition to hold noble silence coming out of a quest until you finish with a final sweat lodge ceremony. I wanted to embrace my parents who were there. It was a sweet moment that had come to be, and because I was not caught in any negative thoughts or expectations, all seemed to flow easy, allowing my parents to still make their way to the land and be of support.

Now that everyone who had sat out had all spoken with grandmother, it was time to head into the sweat lodge. On the way into the lodge, my dad asked Grandmother if this was going to in any way go against his religious beliefs. She assured him this would only help to uncover and add to his faith and connection to "God" or "Great Spirit," as spoken in Native American terms. It was interesting to learn that for those having Native American blood, it was rarely encouraged to raise your children to know their roots as a Native American, out of fear that they could be killed.

The first few rounds were easy. My dad, the amazing scientist that he is, wasn't fazed by the heat and was easy with the darkness. When we got to the sharing round, people had shared, and my dad said, "Well, I am here, so let me share something that even my son doesn't know. The guy you all know as Sid is pretty amazing. He has always done things that would surprise his mother and me. Before Sid was born, I was going through my own life moments. I was in a place where I was searching for my own personal healing. I got on my knees and prayed for a prophet. I was sent Sid; he is the prophet that everyone is looking for." I was floored, as I never in my wildest dreams would have thought that once again my parents were supporting me more than maybe they knew. The fact that I went out to sit for my family, and here it was, in one share, I was lifted up to understand how I came to be here in this life.

After the sweat lodge we all went in to have the closing feast. It was nice to sit with my parents and everyone else, and reflect. To sit and feel peace was exactly why I went to sit this time around. I went out to sit so that I could share my energy with those I loved. The amazing thing was, that in the process of this third vision quest, I captured so much peace inside that the whole time I was out, it was as if there were no animals or anyone else that would come to visit me. I captured a sense of peace inside that would create peace on the outside. It was on this quest that I received my Native American name, "Nahi Adanedi Nvwatohiyadv," meaning "He Brings Peace," and my mission: to bring peace to the world. I knew at the end of this quest that there was still work to be done, so that I may walk in a way of love for everyone. I had begun a deep cleansing process, an upbringing of the Nahi Warrior within myself that could stand for peace for everyone else. This was the birth of the "Nahi Warrior" that would allow me to be the peacemaker for all.

Time would come, and I knew I wanted to complete the process. One thing is for sure: I finish a task. I knew I was writing two books, and I had been filling the book of things I had done, far more than the things I had yet to complete. I presented Grandmother with my tobacco to go sit for my last quest. We would talk for months as she would sit to see if I should go out or not, and never received an answer. Finally, the day she would leave to come and pay me a visit, she would go out to the dock before she left and look across to the space where I had gone to sit on my previous quests. She said to the ancestors, "My grandson is going to expect an answer so that he can begin to prepare for his next quest." She said all of a sudden, a deep eerie peace came over her. So much peace that it was deafening. From the deep peace, she said she heard Jesus. She asked again, "Should my grandson go out on vision quest?"

The response she heard was, "He has me, what else could he possibly need?"

I had been a lululemon ambassador for a year and began traveling and teaching various events around the country. I was asked to come to Annapolis to lead a class dedicated to healing the bay and raising money to support the oyster population. It was a great class. I got to work with, and got to know, Amanda, who would later go on to train with me in teacher training and move on to make huge shifts with her husband.

After the class, we went to have breakfast. It was my birthday, and Amanda insisted we go to a restaurant called the Back Porch, which was literally on the porch of a yellow house with a beautiful view of the bay. As we stood in line waiting for a table, Amanda went on to explain how today was the first time she felt safe to om at the end of a yoga class. She said that when I explained that an om was a way to measure the energy flowing through your body and related it to the first word typically spoken by most babies, although we assume it is "mom," that it just clicked for her. As we were talking, a lady overheard the conversation and said that anyone talking about om at breakfast was worth talking to. All of a sudden, we were told that if we wouldn't mind sitting as a group, we could sit in the next ten minutes. We all said this would work, as long as we had room for one more. As we sat preparing to order food, the lady talked about how her friend had a retreat center in Nicaragua and was looking for a powerful partner to come and lead retreats. Amanda nudged me, as she knew one of my goals was to lead a retreat out of the country. We started to discuss the possibilities, as I was stating there are no coincidences in life, I saw my friend who was meeting us for breakfast walk in. As Kathleen joined us at the table, the woman sitting with us looked up at her and said, "Oh my, I haven't seen you in so long, Kathleen." It was a definite sign that we were meant to meet.

So many things began to come clear for me. I no longer wanted to walk through life holding on to anything that would move me away from peace. I began to see that in order to be the love that I want to be in the world, I would need to be ready to hold an unshakable peace in every way. I knew that I would be able to go back and spend time with Baron in a new space after we had gone our separate ways some time back. I reached out, and he welcomed me back to assist him as he led trainings. Since it had been six years since I last attended a training,

I would need to come and attend a program first, in order to be able to come and assist. He offered me to come to the next retreat in Mexico. I would just need to cover my lodging and travel. I looked forward to seeing him again and where everything was, and just be in the space with everyone.

When I arrived in Maya Tulum, Mexico, I went and got set up for the first workshop. As I walked in, I was greeted by one of the teachers. Phil and I had been through many trainings, and I had been in his studio several times in Rhode Island. What was strange to me was the first thing that came out of his mouth was, "What are you doing here?"

I responded by saying, "I thought I was here for the training." I could see how my mind was watching everything to see what it would be like. I knew if I stayed stuck in the past, I would never experience peace in this moment. Somehow, I was looking to move forward and just be at ease in every way.

Later that evening we went into a community circle. The community circle was designed to clear any conflicts, personal accountabilities, and to acknowledge people for special actions. As we started to move into the conflict part of the circle, I could feel my nerves building. I knew in order for me to have peace, I was going to need to move this forward. So, here we go, in front of one hundred and thirty people, I was going to clear this up. I stood up, and I voiced my conflict. Clearing all the story that was attached, I said, "When I was called and told that I would no longer be considered an affiliate studio, I felt hurt, sad, and angry." There was nothing more to say. I stated what I saw from my perspective. I was clear on that, no matter what the response was going to be. I was going to be okay, and move forward. It was the simple space of being heard, and I didn't necessarily intend on it being heard by one hundred thirty people, and I was called to get clear right then and there.

One of the assistants stated that they wanted to respond. Baron reached over and said, "No, I need to respond." We made eye contact, and he responded with, "Doesn't fit."

I must say, I did not follow his response, and that really didn't matter. I had a choice to spend the next seven days miserable or be at peace. I chose peace, and from this day forward,

I would choose to have peace no matter what happened on the outside.

I woke the next morning, and I was really fired up to have a great day. I was given a copy of my friend's new album, "Light Inside You," by Govindas and Rhada, before it had even been released. Over the next several days, I would listen and sing along and bask in the peace and joy that it stirred inside me. When we went to practice, I felt powerful and alive. Everything was free and full of ease. I really had nothing to hold back. Care free, I was present and here for me, and it made absolutely no difference what was to come next. I was grounded in the moment. Later that day, I was walking the beach, I could see Baron in the distance, coming my direction. We were both being stopped by people along the way, until space opened up, and we were standing alone. We began to talk. Baron brought up my clearing to check in and make sure I was okay. He went on to explain how he was seeing what I was going through in my divorce. Everything was taking place in divine order. He assured me that he thought that for me to be at ease, it was best if we parted ways for a time. I understood, and I explained that I was hurt because I had felt that I had lost a friend.

He then said, "Well, here we are. That was the past. We can leave it there if you want." And that is exactly what we did. We would go on to have a great week, and I would get to see my reflection in everyone around me and continue to move forward.

Some time would pass, and we would continue to cross paths as we walked through parallel lives. At this point, I was doing many different things. I had joined a team of yogis and began teaching once a year at the Easter Egg Roll during President Obama's second term. I got to know some great people in that process. I would also begin to deepen my connection to making music. Everything was beginning to flow in a much grander way. I was invited to bring someone from my staff with me to Park City, Utah, so that we could go to Baron's affiliate studio convention. It was nice to visit and see what everyone was up to. I also would have a chance to connect once again with my friend. It is a great space to be in, to gather with a large group of people reaching for a common goal. We would practice, share lessons and stories, and get recharged, to all continue to do what we did best, teach yoga.

On the second day, I had a feeling I just couldn't shake. What was coming up for me was the fact that my son Sid had recently injured his foot playing football. He was in his senior year, and going into the season, we anticipated him playing well to earn a scholarship to play college football. With his injury, he was out for four games. During this time, I was reflecting on how I had helped twenty-three players make it, not only to play in college, but to go on to play in the NFL. Here, I was at a point where I felt defeated. I was able to help so many, and right now, I felt helpless that I couldn't help my son.

As I shared this with the group, Baron looked up at me and said nothing. It was different for him to remain quiet, yet it was no big deal to me. One of the facilitators helped me move through the moment with the group. I felt better.

Baron then stood up to tell everyone he would be gone for the remainder of the convention. He was leaving because his eldest son was having ankle surgery on the same foot, from an injury playing football as well, and was going to miss the rest of the season. As Baron was leaving, he came over to apologize for not having any words to say. It was a moment that we were both able to pause and see just how parallel our lives were moving.

Both of our sons healed in many ways and moved forward with their lives. For me, I was able to see my son from a different place. I could see that as he was moving forward, I could help to release some of the father/son tension that had come with raising and being the eldest. It was time for me to see how I could hold a space for him, to help him move into his own legacy easily and gracefully.

There are so many places where we all can find an opening into a deeper understanding of our own journey and life in general. I am grateful, not only to have had so many people and experiences that have helped me shed light on mine, but also for the places and faces they lead me to next, to further my understanding.

Another person who communicated a higher vibration for me, came at just the perfect time. After going through several shifts, I was looking for a connection to understand my soul's journey. Where did it all start? I began to dive deeper into a yogi's journey, and for me that meant asking over and over, *who am I?* I would find a person who could make contact and communicate with the spirits, a medium of sorts, who would help me connect more dots. A medium is an individual who uses his or her psychic abilities to see the past, present, and future. I began to hear just where it all started for me. This understanding helped me to become more comfortable with the trials I had faced, knowing that I was evolving to be everything I was meant to be. It helped me to see that I came for a reason, and that reason was to continue to fulfill my mission. I began to see that for me to maintain and carry on in peace, I would have to help others find peace in their lives as well.

In the spring of 2013, I took some people to Nicaragua for a retreat. It was a special place I had flown to a year prior. I went to see the property for a yoga video we were shooting. The locals told me there was a Shaman who wanted to see me and give me some information. It was a pretty good distance to drive to get to the location where the Shaman was. We only had a two-hour window before he would be leaving. When we arrived, there were at least fifty people there, waiting to speak with him. Soon after, an assistant of his came out and said to me, "Our Shaman will be right with you." I felt bad, as I felt like I was cutting in line. What made my time more valuable? I went over and apologized to one man. He said, "Don't worry, I am waiting for him to tell me it is my time to die. I am ready to leave."

I went in to see the Shaman. We had a pleasant exchange of energy. I did not understand their language, and an interpreter was there to help guide me with what was being said. The Shaman pulled cards out and began to tell me about my life. He first talked about how I am supported and loved by the gods and how I was sent here to do great work on this earth, that if I chose to do my work in Nicaragua, it would be well received, and that no matter where I chose to do my work, it would be profound and incredibly impactful, reiterating that the gods are excited and ready to support me in every way. He paused and asked who the woman was that was with me. I told him her name was Lindsay and that she is a very kind person. He asked for her birthdate. He looked at her and then me and said, "This will not work. It will not work because there will be jealousy. There will be moments to come, and you will shift to see things differently." I understood what he spoke of, from all that I had witnessed as I checked in with myself over the years. I saw how nothing I ever thought about another was ever anything more than my perception, that no matter what, everything is seen from my own eyes, and I can shift that view at any point in time. He spoke of how I would end up with someone who was a Sagittarius and how she and I would do many things together that would shift the world. Our love would shine through and allow others to see just what love would be.

The last thing he shared was to advise me to stay away from dairy during my visit there. I had already had cheese during my stay, which resulted in an upset stomach. I decided to heed his warning signs and refrain from consuming cheese or any other form of dairy while in Nicaragua. By the time we would shoot the yoga sequence video for the Nahi Warrior flow, my stomach would be clear.

From my very first visit, Nicaragua felt as if it were a place I had visited in a previous life. There was just something so familiar about it. When I returned the second time for the retreat, I felt like I was home. The people who worked there remembered me and welcomed us with great warmth and hospitality. We had a really great group of people in attendance for the retreat. Everyone was going through something different. One person came with her sister; they would both shift as we moved through the week-long program. Another person would connect on how, as she moved from a separation with her husband, everything would be okay, and she and her daughter would live a life they enjoyed. One person was searching for what was next in her career. She was a yoga teacher searching for what was next. It was great to help her realize she could stand for herself, open up a studio, and later see she and her sister go on to light up Nashville, touching lives and moving people's souls.

Liz was also on this retreat, and it was great to see her begin to open up in her practice and begin to believe in herself. At this time, she and I were in a much different space than where we would eventually end up. It was great to help her realize her own potential. She would go on to teach and we would begin a great friendship.

There were so many great moments while on this trip. One in particular was when we all got to swim in the lagoon with all the small fish. It was awesome. Eventually everyone got out except for Liz and me. We stayed in and talked for some time. This really was a great trip, as it would mark another new beginning I would later discover. We closed the retreat with a fire ceremony. It was a perfect ending to a great new space.

We have a soul's record from the moment our soul is incarnated; this is called our Akashic records. The record carries everything that has ever taken place as our soul moves through all of existence. The existence of such energetic records has been known by people worldwide and is called by various other names, including the "Book of Life" in the Bible. The further we look back, the more we will realize that we truly are all from the very beginning of time. Some of us may have broken off farther from the initial source than others, yet we are still from the same source.

I would spend a year working with my friend, Sallie Keys, a healer who clears Akashic records. As I began to dive into my records, I came to understand many moments that were hitting me energetically before I was even aware them. There were times I would feel I was getting upset, and I'd have no clue where it was coming from, or other times when I would feel a deep sense of hurt or sadness that would linger and even sometimes, take days to move through. My clearings would respond almost instantly. At one point, she told me she had cleared all negative attachments from my past lives, as well as from my current life. What really blew my mind was fifteen minutes after she had said this, I received a phone call from my second ex-wife. It would be one of the most amazing and healing conversations I would have to date. She called to say that she wanted to clear our relationship and acknowledge what was good in our time together. She also pointed out how she felt inauthentic at times and spoke on how in order to have an authentic relationship, both people must be in a space of authenticity.

The clearing of my Akashic records helped me to realize there were a few things left to add to my list. I realized that as I would do this, some things would likely change the course of my life once again. I began to further see just where I was still not aligned to what I wanted. I began to watch and question the relationships all around me. My relationship with my wolf, Shiva, would reflect how I moved from one space to another. I came home one day to realize just how heartbreaking it was every time I looked in Shiva's eyes, as she waited for me to let her out of her crate. I related it very much to the space I was living in at that moment. I found myself living from a space of feeling trapped. It didn't matter who would understand, I knew it was time for a shift. I knew when I could allow Shiva to find her freedom to roam and enjoy the life she knew in her heart, I would be free as well. I began to see how I could further release the conditions around me that would free us both.

I started having deeper conversations with everyone around me. I spent time releasing my defensive stance in life, to let go of the need to protect myself, and open up to a greater love than I had realized could be tapped into. I recall, upon returning from a trip, a conversation with Liz, who was watching Shiva while I was away. She explained how she had never cared for a dog before; somehow I missed this awareness initially, considering I just left Shiva in her care, and how when she tried to put her collar on, it would just hang loose over Shiva's head. So on their walks, Shiva would pull forward so that the collar would stay on. As they returned back to the house, Shiva would put on the brakes and pull back for her collar to pop off. Shiva stood, looked at Liz, and sat down. This was a game Shiva would play as she saw Liz as an extension of the pack.

Liz said as soon as she approached her, Shiva would take off. Liz said her first thought was, "Oh my gosh, Sid will kill me. I just lost the wolf, let alone the little dogs in the neighborhood that could now be in trouble as well." After chasing Shiva around, in what felt like a panic-stricken nightmare for Liz, and for Shiva, a playful game of chase and frolic, Liz finally gave up. Liz said she sat and looked at Shiva, and spoke from her heart, asking Shiva to please come back. Liz said, in the moment, it seemed as though Shiva felt bad for her and made the decision to end the game. Shiva was great at teaching how to let go of control, and open up to ease in the moment.

Liz and I would go on to talk more and discover that there truly is more to life than we both knew. My personality is to reach out to live life, and see all possibilities. The traditional is just not the path I have walked. I explained how we are given the reigns to life, and the greatest gift I can give another is to "choose" to be with them, to stand with someone just because I want to be there.

Love for me, is love. I love everyone fully. I will love, and that is it. Most people would resist this conversation and miss my point because of the conditions that they desire to live within their life. We all live from different concepts and our own perspectives, and for me, I live from my concept of being love for all. This was not always the case for me, but this is where I stood then, where I stand now, and where I will stand until I leave this planet.

Liz responded with a statement that took me into a deeper reflection. She stated that as long as someone would love her fully, and could come home, and be love, she would stand in love always. From that moment, I began to watch Liz from a different view. I wanted to see, could there really be someone who truly understood where my heart was moving? Could there be someone who was truly just love? I began to see and understand just what was being shown to me. My reflection was moving into love, and I no longer needed anyone's approval, other than my own.

After my return from Nicaragua, Grandmother came to town to lead a course. We started with thirteen people, and everyone was eager to dive into a huge spiritual shift. Grandmother was the first teacher to teach "A Course In Miracles," before it had even become a published book. We would go through the course for a year as a group and see just what was to come of it for each of us. I noticed as we moved through each day, I was being led through lessons one day before the lesson was presented within the book. Just like other teachings I experienced, I was being guided along this journey before it would take place. All was coming forward in a grand way. This weekend, Grandmother would also give me the information about my fourth quest. As we sat to discuss it, she shared that she was told that I should wait another year for vision quest. That I should sit in the people's lodge and meditate for four days instead. She said I could have food brought to me, but I needed to sit and go in.

The first day of my four-day meditation, I began to write a letter to Jesus. I asked if he would come and tell me what I was meant to do, and that if he would come, I would follow everything he wanted me to do. If he did not come through, I would go on with my mission and make sure that I fulfilled everything I set out to do. I sat and I waited.

All of a sudden, I heard a sound. The sound I heard was indescribable. It seemed like I was sitting under a jet plane, but even louder than that. It was so loud, to this day I have no way of describing something I have never heard before that has no comparison to anything. What I do know is when I went to look out the window, I saw a black sky, yet it was a perfectly clear night to where the sky should have been filled with stars for as far as the eye could see. I could see one giant sphere where there were no stars, then outside of that sphere, were stars. After the sound faded away and the stars filled the sky, I felt as if there was a presence left behind. Although I was in shelter, I still felt alone, as no one else seemed to wake up or be alarmed from the sound that had just shaken the entire lodge.

When morning came, I was truly exhausted. I had just experienced what was beyond my scope, and now I must sit and reflect. I reflected on and off throughout the day. I even briefly sat with the thought that maybe the elders were playing a joke on me. I knew one thing, and that was I was still moving forward on getting clear on my mission and how it would play out.

As nightfall came, I still had this feeling like there was something there. Before it got completely dark, I would open the front door to the lodge, walk around outside, and look to see who or what was there. Again, I asked for a sign that Jesus was there. I was ready to live out whatever he wanted me to do. Again, I did not receive a message. I sat and began to reach for a deeper peace within myself.

All of a sudden, I heard huge footsteps walking toward the building. Now I have seen some interesting things, and I have heard some far-out stories from the elders of the land. As the footsteps got closer, I began to move away from the door. I looked out the window to see if anyone was up in any of the other lodges. All the lights were off. Something came to the door and jiggled the handle. The door did not open, then something pulled on the door with such force, that it sounded as if it was about to be pulled right off its hinges. Whatever it was, it gave up when the door did not open. Again I would not get any sleep, and I would have to sit and wait for the night to pass so I could speak to Grandmother.

Once everyone had awakened, I went to find my grandmother so we could check in on my experience and we could leave. I explained to her what came to me. She asked what I thought it was. I told her I felt like the first night was a ship of some sort. She nodded yes, and went on to explain their ability to cloak when they come into our atmosphere and how they are unable to imitate stars, so that would explain why it looked like a black void above me.

The second explanation was a little harder for me to wrap my head around, as I was still just trying to process in my mind and find acceptance of what took place at this point. Grandmother continued on, explaining that there are beings that can land and survive in any atmosphere. "When someone has gotten as far as you have with discovering this level of peace, they want to know what you are doing. This being is sent to sit with the person, to see just what was taking place. It is always a peaceful exchange." Grandmother went on to explain that our people have been sitting with beings from other worlds for as long as we have been around. Everyone in the universe is seeking the highest connection possible, that is why they want to know you.

After this experience, it was now time to complete my journey of four. I would prepare over the next year to go out and discover what was to come. Part of my preparation was taking a group of people over to the Big Island of Hawaii for a retreat. We got to experience the land and open up to a new energy of the islands. One morning we went for a hike, and as we were walking, I began to feel the group falling behind. As I paused to look back, I notice one of the participants was down on the ground. She was having a panic attack and couldn't breathe. Everyone had huddled around her, as many were beginning to panic. Once I got everyone back, I then began to work with her. I adjusted her legs and then ran energy from my hands to her abdomen. After some time, she began to breathe again. Once she felt better, we got up and left. This would go on to become one of the first of many times I would start to help others heal in some way.

It was at the Rama Shalla retreat center, where we stayed, that I would learn more ways to enhance my meditation practice. Chuck is the caretaker for the center. He and I developed quite a bond. We would wake up every morning before the participants and work on *prana* meditation techniques. I would use these techniques for many years to follow. A few days later, we would take a hike as a group out to the volcano Pee Lei. We drove out to the lava and were going to hike four miles to get to the actual volcano.

It was pretty amazing to see that people had intentionally built houses on the lava, knowing that if the volcano would happen to erupt again, they would leave for a period of time and then come back and build another house. On the Big Island, there is one family that has never been affected by the active volcano. The Kaawaloa family land has been spared for over thirty-five years. The hot lava has only ever made its way to their driveway. They have been teaching their kids for years, if you respect the land and love her, she will love you back. The story goes, whenever she gets ready to erupt, they gather around for a meal and pray. They are teaching their kids that when a guest arrives and wants to come into your home, you welcome them in. So this is exactly what they do. This was a great reminder for me, as I know how my prayers are answered, and have been since I was a child. Faith is through your actions; it is what we can all move to. How you speak, think, and move through life will continue to show whether you have faith or not, in all that is.

Our journey out to Pee Lei was hard, and yet fun. As we walked across the lava, we had to be careful. When you slipped, it was like falling into a thin layer of glass. Stepping with precision was important. I had several cuts when we finished the journey. It took us close to two hours to walk out. I remember being told that God actually resides in the middle of earth and has been sending things up to the surface so that we are able to live out here. I saw how looking up or outside yourself continues to separate us from what is actually taking place. When we look within, we will land in our hearts and open up to the infinite within. To watch the lava come out, from inside the earth, and spill into the ocean, building new earth, caused me to look deeper into what I believed was true. It was time to find a knowing that could not be denied. It was truly incredible to witness the lava flow and then be able to stand on it moments after.

As the sun began to set, we figured it was time to head out. It got dark about forty minutes into our hike back. There were no lights, with the exception of our flashlights and the moon, forcing us to walk slower. Then to add to the fun, we were hit with a steady downpour. Yes, lava like glass and wet, is slick. I began to feel like I was on vision quest with others. I was walking fast to be the lead for the group, when I realized some people were moving extremely slow. I would slow down, and move to the back. That journey would challenge many, and we were no different. It brought several in the group to tears. By the time we made it back, everyone was excited and happy to have made it through a tough journey.

After the retreat was over, I stayed an extra day and got to know Chuck a bit more. We talked about vision quests and how they related to the journey to the volcano. He was intrigued and decided to make the journey over to the mainland, to be there to support me as I went out on my final quest. He said he had never felt the peace that he felt around me, except for when he visited the Mahatma Gandhi Temple in India, so he wanted to come and be a part of my experience.

In the Native American tradition, I was taught early on that the number four was very sacred. In space, we can see the four directions, and from the four cardinal directions, north, west, east, and south, blow the four winds. In time, we see there is sunrise, midday, sunset, and midnight. In the seasons of the year, we have four: spring, where we plant what we want to come; summer, where we cultivate and open up to the joys of life; fall, where we bring what was planted and reflect on what came to be; and winter, where we look to go in, rest, prepare, and gear up for what is to come. In the stages of living, we have our early years, our youth, adulthood, and our elder years. Finally, we have four parts of living: come into our body in a strong way, develop a clear precise mind, open up to a pure spirit, and look after all beings on earth, especially our people.

A few days would pass after the retreat in Hawaii, and it would be time to gear up for my last vision quest. This time around, I was connecting to the deep peace that was spoken of before. I now came into an awareness of not only walking this path, but leading it. It was seeming that for me to go all the way, there was not a person to follow. I had found several people who had helped me to elevate in many ways. I had met many souls moving in parallel walks. Yet for me to go where I desired, I would have to lead my own way. This was a constant revelation that continued on, again and again. A leader is someone worthy to be followed; I would continue to look at me, discover what was worth following, and uncover what I would leave behind.

My fourth vision quest allowed me the space and time to look deeper in my own heart. To see what it was like to walk the Red Road, the road less traveled by man, the road of seeing my reflection in all, the road to seeing the divine energy and how it courses through everything. To see a mosquito is my friend, to see its value as life, and learn to be at ease in every moment, from the tiniest of tiny, to the grandest of grand. It is this walk that I continue to this day, as a peacemaker.

Vision quests create shifts, and as the elders had informed me before, it may take at least seven years to expand for all the lessons to open up. I have had many moments since my last quest, and some are still opening up since my first quest. It is all the moving forward and the many relationships experienced with the many people that have moved in and out of my life, that has led to so many of these shifts. One major shift is a result of the many openings that had come forward from the exchange of energy that had taken place with all the animals and nature in every vision quest. It has been amazing, as my energy has expanded, to watch and see how connected we all are to each other and every being on the planet. I have had moments where spirits have come to me in many forms, in the form of good friends, animals, total strangers, or entities that have visited through ceremonies, meditations, and more.

There were many moments that I would sit, watch, and dive into what was opening for me and for those around me. One of these moments was when we took people out, for the first time, on inner quest. Inner quest was a smaller version of vision quest. It would allow for everyone to experience sitting out, and to begin to walk a path of deeper awakening. I would see how many things would grow in me as I would help others. I began to see how connection to Spirit would show as people would sit out. Many of my personal experiences would show up with others, and I would be able to relate and open up to intuitive hits to help share from my experience with their overall process. The things people would experience would range from visits from the animals, to hearing voices from the unknown, to seeing me appear, or having deep conversations with so many amazing *Siddhis* (yogic powers) that would come. What we found is that people would have experiences in a day almost the same as those sitting out for several days. The more open a person's body would be, the higher the level of their experience would be. This was showing how the ultimate goal of yoga was to get someone open, to be able to meditate, and connect to spirit.

In 2013 I took people to a new retreat space in Sedona, Arizona. It was amazing to have a reason to come back to Arizona. Once I landed, I picked up a car and drove to Scottsdale, Arizona. I figured I had two days before everyone else was to arrive, so I could head over to see Alleyah. I went into every store on the block. No one had heard of her or the shop; there was not a single vacancy, and every store claimed they had been there for years. This was truly mind blowing. For years, I had been living with the connection that was made with this woman all those years ago. The woman that would initiate the discovery towards me understanding my purpose and the connection to my spirit, my highest self.

The retreat would go on to be spectacular. I had landed, and this was the time for me to stand for others in a really big way, to trust that I am exactly who I am meant to be, and to hold this space for all. I went on to learn so much while being in Sedona. I learned about how the original owner of the retreat center had contracted a rare disease. He only had a few months to live and had bought the land so that he could spend his last moments having a quiet place to feel at peace. He realized that he had a lot of stuff, and that this was a young age to have no one to leave it to. He didn't have family, and he knew it was a waste to hold on to all of it. He would go out to the field and sit and watch the mountains as the sun would set. In Sedona, you don't watch the sunset, you watch the mountains in front of the sun, to absorb the breathtaking beauty of colors that would dance across them. He would sit and contemplate his life. He started to give away the things that he had owned. He gave away his helicopter, his jet, and properties—when all of a sudden, he started feeling better.

So then he kept doing it. He would give away something different every day and would continue feeling better every day. Soon enough, he'd outlived his death sentence. He finally reached out to the doctor that told him he was on his way out. The doctor was intrigued and wanted to see him. When he went to visit the doctor, he was told that whatever he was doing, he should keep doing, because it was saving his life. So he did, and went on to live for many, many years. He went on to create the "Release Technique," a method to give away the things that were attaching to your body in order to find a way to live something new. I found this to be incredible, and for years to come, I would see just how that would impact my life as well.

I also learned of a story of how they brought children to the middle of the desert nearby so that they could build a lake. In Japan, they had trained kids to understand how they were connected to different elements. They brought in several children that were connected to the water element. All the kids would go and walk the land. Finally, one young boy felt something and claimed the location where the water would be. They dug and dug, until eventually, they hit a spring which then formed a lake. What I learned from this was that we all have an opportunity to connect much deeper. Once we get connected to whatever that element is for us individually, there becomes so much more to discover. We all have an infinite source inside, and it's up to us to figure out how it wants to express itself.

Sedona will forever be dear to my heart, because it allowed me to see so much about myself. It was easy to understand how this is the most visited place of spiritual leaders around the globe. The energy that comes through all the vortexes is one that allows you to have a direct line of energy in and out of the earth. When you pray, when you think, when you sit and meditate, you dial into something greater than oneself. Sedona solidified that for me even more.

Another sacred place that I had the chance to visit while in Sedona was Cathedral rock. As you look upon it, you can see two beings standing on the top of the mountain. The story goes that there was a couple who were arguing. God took them aside and had them stand at the top of a mountain with their backs to one another. As you look at the mountain, you can see on one side, a man who is looking into a valley. He says he sees the mountains and the colors that shift across them as the sun sets. He is able to see such a stunning view that it is absolutely undeniable. On the other side and to his back, is his wife. She would go on to describe what she saw. The trees, the running river, and the animals were sheer beauty to her eyes. God asked, "So, who is right?" Was he wrong for what he saw? Was she wrong for what she saw? It truly was just a perspective. What was important for each of them to understand is that they are just seeing from their own eyes, and perspectives change in any given moment. So to learn to love and stand for one another, they would have to let go of holding on so tightly to their individual perspective.

I began to look back and connect the dots of moments that had passed in my life. I would flash through and begin to understand how my energy was ignited. I once was visited by a man who said he had a message for me. He delivered that message by sitting in meditation with me. I could see the transfer of energy through my mind's eye. He would tell me how he was visited in his dream by Swami Muktananda, who said he needed to deliver Shaktipat to me so that I would open up to bring things forward for so many to see. Shaktipat is the conferring of spiritual "energy" upon one person by another. This is truly an act of grace.

I would later go on to study for a couple years with Swami Muktananda's head bodyguard. She would guide my second wife and me weekly, as we were moving through deep openings during our meditation practice. When our time came to an end with her, I took away an understanding that I would eventually be able to make it to my fullest expression possible. I also learned in my time with her the realization that just because I shift me, may never mean another person may shift themselves as well. Simply put, if they desire to remain and play in the same game in their life, they will find someone else to play it with. It was amazing for me to come to this realization, to truly see that I had cleared my Akashic record, and how making this connection in my understanding would create a shift in my relationship with Lindsay. I realized something on the list was missing for me. It was my search for the partner in me. Over the years, I continued to see that for me to land fully in the expression of my highest self, I would attract a partner I would go on to walk with for many moons to come. The missing piece was an understanding of my fullest alignment to my spirit's depth.

Once again, as it goes, I would find that when I am in the flow, whatever I need to elevate me comes in exactly as needed. A friend sent me an article on Quantum Healing Hypnosis. This was great, because I knew if I could see my past, I could truly understand how and why I am operating here in this life today. I contacted Karen Willis, a licensed hypnotherapist, and she seemed excited to guide me through my journey back. She let me know what would take place in order to move through the journey, and for the next thirty days, she instructed me to write down questions that I wanted answered from my highest self. I would go deeper in my own discovery of what I was seeking to know. I wanted to know just who I was. I wanted to know who I was meant to walk with. I wanted to know how and who I had journeyed with. Once I arrived in Karen's office, I began to sense how I was already moving deeper within. We sat and talked at first so she could get to know me a bit. I felt easy with Karen; I knew I was safe. She was well prepared. A video camera was set, as well as an audio recording as backup, to document the next four hours.

As soon as I sat in the chair for hypnosis, I was out immediately. I would later go back and listen to the recording to confirm this. It was crazy to hear me snoring, then talking, and then right back into snoring. Karen started by taking me into a guided meditation and walked me into a deep space. I started out floating in the clouds, then drifting back, and back, and back in time to where I suddenly began to see a clear vision of moments once lived. I saw myself flying in a ship, a flying saucer to be exact. I landed the ship in an ocean here on Earth, and I began to swim as I transformed into a dolphin. This was interesting to me, because just a few days before this session, I had a photo shoot with lululemon at the National Aquarium in Baltimore. It was an incredible experience. We got to do the shoot with the dolphins there. At one point, I was doing a forearm stand, and the dolphins began to swim frantically, faster and faster, then leaped out of the water, creating a splash of water towards me, as if they were trying to get my attention. From that moment forward, they would watch me intently. The trainer said, "They are smart and are very curious about you for some reason. You seem to have their undivided attention." I thoroughly enjoyed the moment in connecting with them.

In the second part of the hypnosis journey, I would come to Earth in the same ship. This time, coming out of the ship, I walked onto the shore and was greeted by a woman and her tribe. It was evident she was the queen, the elder of the tribe.

She was there to greet me and show me we would walk this lifetime together. It was a long, beautiful life. I was the same age as she, yet I had the ability to shapeshift, so I never truly aged in the traditional sense. After her death, I would go back to my ship and leave again.

The next portion of the journey revealed I was a seer for a tribe of people on Earth. We were Warriors. Karen asked who was the friend that was with me. Energetically, I recognized him as my present-day friend, Rick. Now, Rick and I have always been connected, from the very beginning. Maybe us connecting in previous lives would explain why. We have moved through our current life on a parallel walk. This would evolve even after I left coaching. We have always remained connected, sharing and reflecting on many of our life's moments. Our spiritual walk has been the biggest connection. We often bounce moments in our lives off on one another. Many of my teachings have evolved out of our conversations. I had kids a bit earlier than Rick. Our older boys are both of our namesakes, and I have seen how we have both experienced many of the same growing moments. It is such a blessing to have a best friend that moves through life on the same trajectory, we are truly able to stand for each other, one hundred percent. Anything ever spoken was safe, and it allowed us to appreciate that we had another's perspective outside of just one path of life experiences. We continue to connect the dots today.

Living as a "Warrior," I was a witness to see the Spaniards land and how our people were forced out. I witnessed how, at the core of me, I did not want to fight. That has always held true in my current life as well. I have always known there is another way, yet if called to make a stand, I would ride with my people until the end. I saw how anger caused an accident, and I felt that pain deep within as it was revealed that I lost my best friend in battle during that lifetime. Whether it is this life, one before, or one to come, I am blessed to know and believe that I am and will be connected to Rick for all our days to come. Our ministries may look different to the outside world, yet we both know we are traveling the road of life side by side.

I then went back to my ship and left Earth once again. Once I reached outer space, I attached to a space station to see and speak to all of the beings that came aboard this vessel for a formal meeting. I was the speaker of this universal council. I would go on to explain that Earth was not ready for peace, that it would take time. The council asked what Earth was like. I said, "It hurts. It hurts in my chest and in my heart." The feeling would come in as I began to bring more of my spirit's essence into my current physical body, sitting in Karen's chair. I was able to let the feeling pass. There was an uproar in the council after stating I was not going to return to Earth. One of the leaders protested, "You asked for this, and now you want to back out?" I would eventually accept the mission and agree to go back in time. At this point, Karen dialed in and realized where I was. She asked to speak to my subconscious. From my subconscious, I knew everything that had ever been before. Karen was extremely kind and cautious in speaking to me. She began to ask questions as I moved deeper. My answers began to get distant. There would be long spaces in between my answers. I began to speak in one moment as I, and another in the third person.

Q: Does Sid need to intake more food to take care of himself?

A: He needs to eat fish, rice, and potatoes. He needs to get rid of meats.

Q: Am I speaking to Sid's subconscious?

A: Yes.

Q: Do I have permission to speak to Sid's subconscious?

A: Yes.

Q: I respect the power of the subconscious because I know that the subconscious takes care of Sid's body and does a very good job of it. I know that the subconscious has a record of everything that has happened in this lifetime or any other lifetimes he has ever lived, and I respect the power of the subconscious and always ask permission to speak to it and ask questions. Do I have permission?

A: Yes, you can speak.

Q: I know the subconscious could have brought forth many different lifetimes, why did it choose to bring this one forward?

A: Because it is who he is now, it is who he needs to be for the world. He is here to help everyone, and he is doing great work. He can speak and stop holding back.

Q: What level is the subconscious on now?

A: The level he is letting through.

Q: Can he go deeper?

A: Yes.

She invites in a higher level.

Q: Is he to bring about a new religion that will heal him and the world?

A: A new way of living, that leads to a deeper faith.

Q: Is this a type of religion?

A: Just show them how to live. He teaches himself as he teaches another. He is good at checking in. He teaches with integrity because he checks in with what he tells someone because of the way he knows how to live his life. He knows beyond doubt.

Q: He wants to know, how can he live with his higher self on a daily basis?

A: Stop thinking! (Laughter ensues.) Sounds easy, doesn't it? He used to live this experience as a child, to where it was overwhelming when he would leave this portal. He can travel and remain when he drops into his heart, breathes, and asks to get here. Tell him to sit down. Like all the time, stop and sit. Empower them more.

Q: What integrity should he access to heal the world?

A: Unconditional love. He still has conditions. He can't see them yet, because he hasn't gone to those places, those parts of the world. I am still opening him up. He is getting it and will eventually lead all to see that in letting go of their conditions, they will be able to access everything. They will be able to birth something new. With conditions mankind will never change. He will write a book, tell his story of this lifetime. He will access all through athletes. This is a way to get everyone to listen because they won't get caught up in worrying about their religions or their belief systems. People on earth look up to athletes. They are strong, yet they don't know who they are either. They all need self-love. Because we've told them, not me, but you, not you, but they have told them what to feel.

Q: They've been taught that? Conditioning?

A: Yeah that word. They've been taught that something about them isn't good enough. Yet everything about them was created by me.

Q: And who is me?

A: Who do you think I am? I am who I am. I am the one connected to everything.

Q: To Sid, to Karen?

A: Yes, you are talking to me, and I am talking to you, and we are one.

Q: Thank you, it is a great privilege. What is it everyone needs to know now?

A: Everyone needs to know that everyone is connected. Everyone needs to know there won't be any peace, if all don't have peace. They won't know me, if all don't know me. Sid is to walk as love. As he walks, people feel it. All he has to do is walk; they will feel it. Do you feel it? (Karen acknowledges yes.) He knew you felt it. He will know all in due time. He can remind himself by listening to this. He will soon understand the profundity and own the ultimateness of who he is. This is where the highest knowledge is. His remembering will absolve him from all doubt.

Karen would spend another hour asking my higher subconscious my questions in the order that I had written them. What was intriguing and would bring about goosebumps for me, when I would later listen back, was hearing the major shift in the vibration and sound of my voice.

Q: What was his relationship with Jesus?

A: He and Jesus are one, not because he is Jesus, but because he and I are one, and because I am one, we are one. He and Jesus "coach" each other. Sid likes that word. He has to ask, and the more he asks, the more he will know. If he gets a concept of where he is in the heart, go deeper. If he can perceive it as not real, go deeper. The more that he goes into this space, the more he will access, and eventually, will just be in this space. When he flows it, he will set up stations. Stations for people to open up. With each relationship, Sid has gone deeper. Closer to understanding unconditional love. All will find it, when they look within.

Q: What did Jesus do?

A: He loved so much, that he loved all. He had trust beyond his fear. He granted himself this trust. He would talk to his father about how he could trust. He would open up his mind to a place so deep within. He was so connected to the infinite, that his trust would manifest anything.

Karen started to guide me back. As I came out of my hypnosis, it would take some time to integrate back into my body and reorient back into the moment. Karen counted to ten. I felt exhausted as I landed back in. I began to stretch and would take some time to visit with her before I would head home. As I left her office, I came out to find two hawks sitting. I knew they were there to remind me of the space I am and to embrace it. I then got in my car and began to drive home. Off in the distance, I noticed two bald eagles sitting in a tree. I pulled the car over and spent time with them. I now knew that this life was sacred because I was here.

This journey has moved me through so many moments. It has been mind blowing to meet so many people that have come in and out of my life, people who could see the past and the future, people who could speak to realms we can't usually see, and people who could see just where your body was off and how to heal it. What's really been special is seeing people who had no clue what gifts they had, and have them be revealed to them. As I lifted my energy, they too would ignite to something new.

One day I got a phone call from a friend, Desmond, a connection I made through a doctor that practiced at our studio. He asked if I would be willing to come to Kingston, Jamaica, and speak to twenty-five men who were convicted and sentenced to death row. Every single man I had the pleasure of meeting seemed to have shifted to a place of wanting to be peace in the world. Each one seemed to truly have a kind heart and a genuineness in wanting to make sure everything was left in a good way. I understand it can be easy for some people to appear as if they look clean, but no one can fake it when it's this deep within. It was amazing to sit with men who were convicted, and about to die, and truly feel brotherhood and experience peace in the moment with them. After speaking with the men, Desmond asked me if I was free to come to a meeting and speak with some people the next night. I was in Jamaica to get to know the land and the people, so of course I said yes. Desmond didn't specify what type of meeting, and I guess I didn't ask. When he picked Liz and me up from the hotel, we were nicely dressed and ready for what we thought was going to be a meeting of a business of sorts. On our way, I began singing in the back seat of the car. Desmond said, "Sid! That is your way, you need to sing and get your message out to the world."

When we got there, everyone was clean and ready for a meeting, but not in the "business" sense. No one was wearing suits, but rather much more casual attire. They asked what would I like to do. I decided to have everyone pull up chairs and come together in a circle. I started by wanting to get to know who was there. I asked if everyone could introduce themselves and share something about themselves. By the time we got to the third person, I realized where we were. We were in a drug rehab center. It came into my awareness how I was unable to see anything but kindness in the hearts of convicts I had sat with the previous day, and now I couldn't even recognize people who were healing from drug addictions. What I saw in every person, no matter what, was their situation, and the sense of hope they had about them. As I sat in listening at the rehab center, I wanted to leave them with something that could help them in their situations. I asked for a dry erase board or chalkboard. They had neither, but they had beautiful white marble floors and a dry erase marker. I love delivering, and one thing is for sure: those who have hit rock bottom, will do anything to find joy. This is where my passion and determination in helping others shift comes full throttle. I had their attention, and I taught like I could save a person's life in a single moment. It brought me joy to hear everyone coming up after, explaining how they understood what I said, and that they would indeed heal from this moment on. Months later, I would receive emails, learning how so many were clean and living well, and updates of how many of the men had gone on to start new jobs and experience their lives in so many new ways. This is what inspires me to live the life that I do.

The next day, Desmond came by to take us to get lunch. He asked what I wanted to do while we were there. I said it would be great to see about finding land or a retreat center to arrange making some things happen there in the future. Desmond said we should take a ride to Ocho Rios. On the way, he insisted that we head over to Gunsmoke to meet with a music producer first. He shared that he loved my voice and would love to help bring this part of me forward. I had put my music down for some time, and this would be a catalyst to bring my singing back. This was truly the birth of the band "Nahi" and many music projects to come.

The next stop was to go by Bob Marley's house. I was inspired by the mark he left on Jamaica and the world, as well as how his legacy would come through his kids, and how his music would survive, all as a result of sharing the convictions in his heart.

We continued to journey towards the coast. Once we arrived in Ocho Rios, we got off the bus and got a ride home to Desmond's old house. He insisted we take a look at an old empty park nearby. We hopped the fence to get to the abandoned property. We walked down towards the water and found there was a man sitting in a truck. We talked as he showed us around the property. He then made a phone call to Ard, the owner of the property. Ard and I spoke, and he said he would like to meet. He said they were looking for a yogi who wanted to help build up the land. The next day we would meet with Desmond in the morning and then meet up with Ard. Ard took us to his property up in the hills. We saw many Buddha statues as we walked to the top of the property. I gazed out into the ocean from the peak of the hill. Suddenly, it hit me: I'd been here before. This was the same view of a recurring dream I had as a child, from nine years old until I was seventeen. During this running dream, I would live out a full life. It would take me from childhood into adult life. I have always known what my home eventually would look like. I have known for many years destiny would have me live with an ocean. Many things continue to add up and enforce me to live that dream in every way. Ard and I stayed in touch, agreeing we'd revisit again in the near future.

I met a dear person who would end up awakening a space deep within me. Never having channeling or psychic abilities prior to this, my friend began to hear voices from a place beyond what she ever knew was possible. What came through, or shall I say, *who* came through, were my energetic parents. We all have earth parents, and I chose to be here on earth with the most amazing people I could, in order to become the person I came to be for the world. I believe we all have energetic parents that were the ignition of our souls. Through my friend, I was able to tap in to hearing from my beginning.

The messages came in as follows:

"Sid, listen. We are here for you. We know you feel that you are okay, and you are, but it is important that you know we are here for you and we love you. Please TRUST us. Have you found that deep trust within? Do you really believe that we are here? If you did, you would see us and feel us whenever you want."

Over the years, I had begun to listen, and in order to listen, you must be able to hear yourself. My answer to this was no, I don't trust. Yes, I do believe they are here. I know I am connected, and it is time for me to see them anytime.

"We are sorry we cannot tell you how to make this flow in with more ease. It is meant to be difficult. It is meant to crack you wide open in order to test your faith. You are strong, stronger than you know. You may not see us until after you have been reborn. Please surrender to the process and all that is coming. We can feel your sadness."

I remember as I heard this, I felt a deep sadness come to the surface. I thought I had connected to me many years before. I began to understand that seven years from sitting on my first quest, to connecting my past lives, to healing and connecting to my family, as well as all my relationships, healing all those brake lines was just about to move me through the energy of this shift in a strong way.

"You are literally transforming. You are rebuilding, every step of the way. Watch and listen to yourself and the world around you. Be so in tune with your presence on the earth that you can see how your footstep creates a vibrational shift. Know yourself. Know yourself. KNOW YOURSELF. More than you have ever thought possible. If you give the transformation the time it needs, the time you need, to rebuild and to learn, you will be an unwavering vessel of peace. There will be no doubt or fear in you and no doubt or fear from anyone else. Your walk will change, the way you look in people's eyes will change. You will see and hear differently, you will feel differently, and you will think differently. Your aura and the energy around you will shift. It is the second coming. Take your time and have patience with the shift. There is an image of you after the shift. When you are in full power, you are golden, with peace exuding from your body. Your mere presence will shift the energy of others, solving any conflict just by standing in your power as a peaceful warrior. No words need to be exchanged. Trust in you. With any doubt or any fear, this ability will be hindered."

I paused and knew that I trusted. I asked, how do I lift the veil?

"Reflections. It probably feels trivial to you at this point, given all the work you have done with this, but watch your reflections. Watch what triggers you to feel less than peace, and see if you have TRULY let that go. The veil is in reference to something you are not seeing about yourself. This creates a block, and then you are unable to grow into your full power. Be at ease with all things, even with yourself, especially in realizing that there is still more to learn about you and things to clear out. I cannot tell you specifically what this is. It is for you to learn. You will feel sadness. Know that it is okay, and know that you are loved in entirety. Our son, it is time for WORK. It is time. Yes, there is more work to be done. Remember. Remember where you came from. Remember your purity. Bathe yourself in that purity, the purity of peace with all things. Are you really taking the time? Know we ask this out of love. Take the time. In all interactions, sit with what people say before you react. Feel the words go into your body as energy, feel the energy shift in you, and then feel again what is necessary to send back in order to keep the frequency of peace. Taking time will be difficult for you, but it is necessary.

One day, there will be a day where you fully open up. It is coming soon. Energy will pour out of you like a waterfall or like fire. You will weep, you may get sick, you will feel a deep pain and hurt. This is the pain Jesus felt on the cross. Know that you are loved and you will be okay. You are being reborn on Earth. Your cells are reforming, everything about you is transforming into your purest, truest state of being. Trust in us. We are here for you. All will not be revealed as it comes. You will need to get to a place of understanding and true wisdom to ask the question that will give you what you need next. This is a serious and lengthy transformation, one not to be taken lightly. Write as you watch yourself during this transformation. Write as much as you can. Write all that you feel, see, and hear. Write all of your thoughts. You are going deeper than you ever have. Continually give thanks for the wisdom you are about to receive."

The space that was shared through the channeling and the meditation had brought so much, full circle. I would go on to see, just as I was told, how all was coming.

During my awakening stages, I would go on to meet two beautiful souls who would come visit the studio on several occasions. They were truly selfless about spreading the word through the Hindu system. What I knew about myself was, I am everything, and anything that allows me to better understand God, I want to know all there is to know. What I discovered as I would study multiple religions is that my God, my father, my essence was far too great to limit it to one God. My God, your God, their God, are all just aspects of the Godhead. So for me, taking the time to understand everyone's perspective would lead me closer to the overall understanding of it. I would dive in for several years working with Hindu deities. Manoj and Jyothi spent time teaching me many aspects of God. Jyothi came and awakened a Ganesh statue we had at the studio and spread the word of Vedanta. She had such a captivating, easy way about her, many would gravitate toward her. Manoj in many ways, was a simple man who would enjoy teaching all the aspects of the archetypes.

There were many ceremonies and moments that brought in peace for me and for all who were seeking. I would call other people in to help bring forward a shift in some way for all. I invited a Hindu priest to awaken a five foot Shiva Morti. Shiva is the third god in the Hindu triumvirate. The triumvirate consists of three gods who are responsible for the creation, upkeep, and destruction of the world. The other two gods are Brahma and Vishnu. Brahma is the creator of the universe while Vishnu is the preserver of it. Lord Shiva represents the destroyer of our imperfections to ensure our spiritual progress. He destroys our illusions, desires, and ignorance. He destroys our evil and negative nature. He destroys our old memories, so that we can move on with the movement of time. He destroys our relationships, attachments, impurities, physical and mental wrongdoings, the effects of bad karma, our passions and emotions, and many things that stand between us and God as impediments to our progress and inner transformation. And in the end when we have made sufficient progress, when we are ready and prepared, and when we are willing to become transformed into light and wisdom without any inner conflict, he destroys death itself. As we sat with the statue and called forward the energy to awaken, I would take my hand to my heart and send my essence into Shiva's heart, infusing it with my energy.

My father studied to be a priest for twelve years. I must say, having been raised by parents who were open to learning benefited me so. I am grateful I have shared in many philosophical conversations with people all over the world. What I found was through the Vedanta, Christianity, Buddhism, African rituals, Native American teachings, and all other religions and philosophies, there was a common theme. All would look to help me land in truth by stripping back what was a creation of man, an interpretation from a limited perspective, of what cannot be understood. It is truly in the experience that we are able to land in all that is, was, and will be.

There were found moments that would show up as peak moments for me along the path of my awakening. What would show up to take me all the way into peace and into vibrating the fullest of myself would be the experience of pain. It would take a lot for me to escape the eighteen ibuprofen a day from the pain of years of sports, in order to feel in my body again. I would have to give up sugar and coffee to land deeper. It would take giving up what was no longer needed in order to find samadhi. I would go on to master peace in so many ways by being engaged fully in the experience of all things. It was in 2006 that I would meet with my dear friend, Joe Lathe, to tell my story on my body through many tattoo sessions. We would talk, shift, and heal many times over. We dedicated my right arm to the teachings of the East, my left arm to the teachings of the West, and my back to the elevation of the energy of the eagle.

I am grateful for pain because it has taken me into myself every time I have gotten caught in thought, or looked to escape the pains of the world. The first major moment of experiencing the pain body with myself came just before Liz and I would head to teach on the east and west coasts of Canada. We first went to Chippewa Thames Reserves, in Ontario, Canada. During my next several trainings, I would learn to stand for others, free of their judgments, and would travel on crutches during our time in Canada. Paul, a friend from the Baptiste community, had brought me into his tribe to lead a training for a week. I volunteered my time, because deep inside I knew, if I could help people from the First Nation transform, I would also be helping me transform in the process. First Nations people are descendants of the original inhabitants of Canada who lived there for many thousands of years before explorers arrived from Europe and called them "Indians." The moment I walked in, we went right into teaching. I chose to give as much as I could in that week, knowing that I may never see most of them ever again. I wanted to deliver everything I could, to leave a transformation that would shift them to their core. This particular time, I would speak about Jesus and his teachings. I would pull out many examples of what his view would be on living from unconditional love. I would touch on how everyone that has any reason to justify not loving another is simply creating a condition, which ultimately is not love. As we would get to a point of connecting more to love, the better my legs would feel. When we would drift away, I would start to lose my legs all together.

What I did not know was there was a seer on the land. The seer and her family had been the ones who saw for the tribe for many generations. Unbeknownst to me, before my arrival, the elder of the land had a vision. He had a vision that Jesus was returning, and now here I, a stranger, appeared before them, speaking of Jesus. I had no clue just what was in store for me in this training, as I was unaware of what all was brewing in the background as a result of my being there. In the beginning of the week, I would have everyone participate in an acting exercise to help pull forward an awareness of always being able to choose how we will express ourselves in any given moment. This exercise caused an uproar when some people started acting like drunk Indians. Mind you, for some reason, I continued to push the envelope here. I had never before, and haven't since, used this exercise.

That night, one of the participants began to speak. She was furious and said she had organized the men on the reserve to bring a war party to take me off the land. We sat and we all talked, diving deep into everything. What we came to was they were upset that I came in, did sacred ceremony by myself, and left it out of the teaching. In the beginning, I had explained that they already had what the world needed, that I was there to awaken them to what lay deep inside. After two hours, the energy had calmed. I would then lead a morning meditation and practice. After, we were going to sit with an elder to share in a peace pipe ceremony.

It was amazing to see how everyone looked up to their elder. They revered her so. As she began to speak, she went right in. She called in the directions, spoke to creator, mother earth, and all of our relations. She gave thanks to me for coming and being willing to stand for our people. She then began to teach all the lessons I had delivered. She spoke of how it would take me coming, and rocking the waters, for them to move what no longer served them. I was floored at how clearly she brought this around. A healing circle was complete. After the ceremony, they all came up and apologized and recognized me as their elder. It was a special moment, as we all connected deep within and came out the other side of it all. We would go on and spend the next few days diving deeper in the principles of teaching and how to weave the teaching of our people into the teaching of yoga. It was truly a moment of bringing together the east and the west teachings of life; and to see the transitions from beliefs, to knowing, was incredible. It has been nothing short of miraculous, to see the continuous growth of many after training.

After finishing a huge transformation in Ontario, we would hop on the plane and head over to Alberta, Canada, to lead another training. We had a six-hour flight where we would take advantage of having a chance to close our eyes for a bit. As we took off, I reminisced about coming to Canada for a lululemon event a few years back. Lululemon had brought in twenty-three teachers from all over to take part in a seminar and open up to what was next for everyone. This trip was awesome, except for getting to Vancouver. There was so much traffic, I ended up missing my flight and thought as a result, I would have to miss the trip. I called and explained my situation. Lululemon was great; they figured it out and said if I could get to DC in two hours to catch a flight, I would still make it. Once I got to Vancouver, I would need to take another flight to get to the island.

Wouldn't you know it, a huge fog blew in, and I was delayed once again. After three hours, the flights were cancelled. I would have to go and stay in a hotel for the night. It turned out to be a blessing, as Rob, one of the executives of lululemon, was still in town and we would get together for dinner. It was a great night; as we sat and shared stories, I got to learn more information about lululemon as a company, their philosophy, and what they wanted to bring forward.

After a great meal and visit, I would head to bed. I lay in bed watching a program about aliens on the history channel. It was awesome—more signs that I was seeing that all made sense for me. I also saw a commercial that floored me. The commercial presented a group of grandmothers sitting around having tea. They were speaking of how one of their granddaughters was having her sweet sixteenth birthday. "Wow, what did you get her?" one of the other grandmothers asked. The woman answered, "I got her a whistle, and will teach her how to use it." They all clapped. What stuck with me as I drifted off was the harm done on children. It sparked an opening for me: the need and want to help all children, even those who were grown now.

In the morning, I continued my journey in travel with my flight being on time for departure. I would then take a bus and a boat to get onto the island. By the time I got there, I was a whole twenty-four hours late. I figured there was a reason for it, so I was happy to just be in the flow. When I arrived at the seminar, a woman named Susan was leading the group through self-inquiry. It seemed as though I walked in with perfect timing. She said, "Sid, would you like to do your pechakucha?"

The pechakucha was a series of slides, where we would tell everyone about ourselves in two minutes. Mine was really about my family, my teachers, God, and Chip Wilson, the founder of lululemon, as he was why I was there.

As I finished, Susan said, "Wow, you are the only one who mentioned God. That is exactly what we are discussing. Can you explain more, what God is for you?"

I said, "Yes, God for me is everything and occupies space, time, and form, and has no beginning and no end. It is why I teach yoga, to get people back and reconnected.

"That is it!" she said, "If you all teach yoga and are not taking people to God, you are not truly teaching yoga." I knew I was in the exact place, at the exact time, I was meant to be there.

That night, I was lying in bed and again turned on the history channel. This time, it was the story of Sitting Bull. I felt my heart pulsing in a grand way. I could feel the love in the moment. I could feel the hands of Sitting Bull on my shoulders. Sitting Bull had left his one headdress in Canada before going back into the states. While we were in Canada, we would spend time doing many personal and community-building exercises. Everything continued to line up, and many moments would come to follow. It was the ride back from our retreat with lululemon that would be the reason I made my way to teach on the reserve.

On our way back, three of us gathered in the back of the bus. One of the people invited, told me how her great-grandfather was a poacher who would walk from the east coast to the west coast gathering furs, how he became friends with Sitting Bull, and how he owned one of Sitting Bull's headdresses. Coincidence? I did not think so. As we continued our conversation, I further talked about my desire to teach to my people, to teach to the First Nation. I was then directed to Paul, and everything came to be. I had another wait to take my flight back home. As I was sitting in my hotel room, I heard a drum beat. I looked out the window and there was a band of my people marching through town. I grabbed my boots and ran downstairs. I went into the crowd and started to listen to their chant. This group was there to march against social injustice. I had a couple hundred dollars, and as I met the leader, I would give him the money from my pocket and make a vow to do what I could to help strengthen our people. I would do what I could to help heal our people who were still in the struggle on the reserves in both countries. That first trip to Canada with lululemon was a catapult of so much to come.

So here we are making our way from the east coast to the west and getting set to lead another training. For me, trainings have always been about more than just helping someone teach an asana class, just like coaching football was much more than just X's and O's. The game, like teaching, is an expression of life. How you play the game and how you practice on the mat are reflections of your life. You must first understand you, in order to help another. In our trainings, I have always desired to help everyone find a higher expression of themselves and elevate their lives in every way. We are truly perfect, and to truly reach this perfection, we must stop thinking that to be human is to be flawed.

As we got to the west coast, I would notice that my legs felt a little better. I would not need my crutches during the day, yet I would experience most of my pain at night. I began to notice the more I would spend time with others, helping and seeing them transform their lives to a new place, the more the pain would come. In this training, as in many of the previous trainings, there were many of people being abused as kids. Now, I have no interest in being someone's parent or therapist. Yet what I see for people is how they operate through their life. It is pretty simple for me, and most people like to make living complicated, or make excuses as to why they continue in their patterns. If something isn't taking you to your highest, I ask why continue with them? At the end of the day, whoever you are, it will take discipline to get you there.

As we went through training, things began to build. We had a person in the group with schizophrenia. There were times they would come out and want to control the room. Now, I am willing to stand for everyone, even if one person is tearing down the group or the integrity of the program. What I found in the group in Alberta was that as long as we stood in our own personal integrity, all would come through. The pain in my body would grow every night. It got to a point where Liz would say she was good on having kids. Taking care of people is a lot. Both on the east and west coast, I was treated through First Nation remedies. I had a raindrop treatment where essential oils were dropped along my spine. This was an old Cherokee treatment that gave relief to my pain. I would learn several remedies that would help me move the pain through my body.

As the week would pass, I would shift into a greater pain. So much that I had to dismiss everyone early, two of the days during that week's training. I couldn't walk the steps, I would slide to come down, and get help to get up. I knew that the more everyone shifted, the more I would shift. As we went in, people shared things that they had never shared. Clearing was much like the release technique. As people gave up their old stories, you could see them heal. As I told my story, the release would always clear me in many ways. By the end of the training, everyone had cleared. I was walking, and it was amazing. We went to a hotel closer to the airport, saw a movie, and went to rest for our journey home. In the morning, I woke and I made a choice to leave the crutches behind and head home.

When we got home, I met with a few people. Doctors had no clue what was going on. All of my blood work came up negative, and I had no desire to keep going down that path. I would start to look outside of the traditional ways. I met with several people and connected to my friend Sonia from Jamaica.

She said it was time for me to lead. She believed that I needed to lead in a much more spiritual way. I needed to begin to open up to holding space for others to move through the journey that I had been on. I would sit and listen once again for signs. I remember on the reserve, they mentioned me leading lodge, pipe ceremonies, and all that would come to me. I knew deep down, it was time to bring "The Warrior's Way" forward for all.

I was getting deeper in bringing more energy down to the earth to share with all I would come in contact with. I would lead, and more, and more people would awaken. When I was leading ceremony, I would feel how the energy would enter in, energize, and lift me up. I also noticed coming down. It would often take time to integrate back in. My pain would teach me how to hold peace at great depths, by moving beyond reactions and into knowing, and how to stay conscious in every moment.

Early in December I would start to feel my physical body shifting. We were attracting a huge buzz around town and were being featured on all the major, local television networks. Throughout, I slowly went from needing crutches to getting knocked off my feet completely. On the 21st of December, I woke up needing to get my boys a ride to the airport to go visit their mom in Florida. I knew I likely wouldn't make it back, as my legs had begun to lock up.

By midday, I wasn't able to lift my hands above my head. The first time this happened in my body, I was grateful it was while we were in Canada, so that my boys did not have to see me in such a floored state. The next day, Rick would call. He had seen me on TV and mentioned how I really wasn't looking like myself. I knew exactly what he meant. I was eating less, and somehow my body was bloated. We were always moving through many of the same lessons, and it seemed that the shifts he was discovering in himself might very well help me. He talked about giving up gluten, which I had given up a couple months prior. I had even given up shellfish for a while. Over time, we would continue to reflect and see what was taking place for the two of us.

Over the next ten days, I would experience so much pain, I thought for sure my heart would stop. At one point, I told Liz,

"If I die, leave me for twenty-four hours before you pick up the phone. I promise, I will be back. Trust me." She agreed, and let it be. I was glad the boys were gone through this ordeal. I wasn't aware that they were worried. Yet, I knew either way, they were good. TD and I had had a conversation before, where I asked him how would he feel if something took me away from this world. He said quickly, "I'll be fine." He looked up and said, "I mean I will miss you, and I will be alive, so I have to keep living." For me death has never been a space to fear, and it was apparent to me from his response that I may have imparted this wisdom to him. I know I came from the unknown, it was good enough to get me here, it must be good enough to return to.

The pain I experienced was well beyond anything I could imagine. Nothing would take the pain away. The only relief I got was to take a nighttime cold and flu medicine just to fall asleep. That worked for about two hours, and on a good night, maybe four. I wouldn't leave the bed at all, except to get to the bathroom. I was blessed that Liz had off for winter break from her job. I would get flashes of information that would guide me to keep the peace. Even when the pain would heighten, if I could keep the peace, it would come in much easier. What would hit most were moments like Christmas Day, when no one came to visit. I was blessed that Liz was there, and yet there was a sense of feeling alone in the moment. When the world was celebrating my brother Jesus, I was feeling down like never before.

On December 28, I would have an appointment with a doctor that would shift my reality. His last name was Hahn and although he had no relation to Liz, I felt it was a sign and would go see him. When we got there, it took me thirty minutes to hobble into his office. As we walked in, it felt like I was in the matrix. There stood Dr. Hahn as an older Asian American man who looked just like a man I once saw in an elevator, who talked to me about my tattoo on my arm and how it didn't mean family, as in my family, but rather "FAMILY," the universal family. I began to get out of my head as he finished speaking to the receptionist while we waited to check in. We turned to sit down in the waiting room and noticed all the chairs sat in a circle, much like a large round table we have at home. No matter where you sat in this circle of chairs, you would not exchange energy with others unless you wanted to. We would choose to purposely look around and be mesmerized by each person in the room.

When it was time for me to see Dr. Hahn, to my surprise, he would enter the room as a much younger man than who I saw in the front of the office. I was thoroughly confused, as he was the only doctor practicing there. He started asking questions that were right in line with questions I asked to get others clear. At one point, he asked about my divorce and kids. This went straight into my heart. I began to shed a tear, unsure if I was just sensitive and vulnerable from all the pain or genuinely emotional.

Dr. Hahn said, "I know it can be a tough spot." He put his finger on my heart and said, "Go in."

I felt all the energy move within and begin to bring ease in my body. He then told me to stand up. Now mind you, I walked in on crutches and could barely move at that. I heard him as he said it again, "Come on over here." I looked in and told myself this was my chance to get up, that all of this was in my head, and it truly was up to me. I stood up and slowly made my way over. He had me get on the table and began to do acupuncture. As he put a needle in the crown of my head, I felt energy begin to flow through my entire body. I would spend the rest of 2016 in bed and watch as it all began to clear in perfect timing for me to conduct and lead a powerful training in early January.

We were bringing forward a training to reach into neighborhoods that really had yet to have access to this level of empowerment. The "Teach One, Reach One" program was a teacher training program that would allow a way in for everyone. For every person that registered for teacher training, we would train someone from the Native American reservation, from a low economical neighborhood, a Military Veteran, and/or a woman who had been through an abusive relationship. We would again go deep into getting anyone clear that wanted to move forward. Our conversations touched on racism, rape, abuse, and more. We moved through some really huge moments, sending big ripples of peace into the universe. The next time I would experience pain that would teach me, was this time post training. It truly was an interesting moment. From here, I had noticed a big shift in my teaching. I could tell when my energy would heighten and would come to know and see that the higher the vibration I held, the more others would raise up as well.

Years ago, I was introduced to a healer that would guide me through past life regression. My sessions would lead us through a life of Ra, as the Egyptian sun god, and a life with Jesus. While in the midst of this session, I would hear her crying. She explained that the light that filled the room let her know of my connection to Jesus. She then asked if she could ask questions of her own, in order to test and verify my answers, which she relayed after the session was over. As she realized that my connection was true, she told me about her soon to be ex-husband who was home packing. She wanted me to meet him and shared how he had been working solely on research of Jesus and Ra for the past thirty-five years. He spent half of his life getting paid to gain as much information as possible.

When we finally talked, he started out asking me why I thought so many people were flocking to me for yoga. I told him that people came to me because I was willing to strengthen my vibration and work on me, that every time I would elevate me, more people would come. He would go on to explain that he understood where I was, and that he could explain a few things. He pointed out how that was the case for Jesus, that when he would show up, people would flock because of the vibration he was carrying. The higher he would go, the more people would come around. This landed for me, as he told me this was what was meant to take place for me. He would leave me with a statement that would fuel me for years to come. "Keep going deeper into you, and continue to strengthen your vibration because it is true, the more you open up to this, the more you will touch people."

Going into my next training, I would have two people inform me of what was occupying my space at that time. My friend Ingrid would take and read my aura picture and let me know that there was a dark space signifying a presence in my field. She warned me that I needed to be aware of all people that I surrounded myself with. I was also told by Sonia, my friend and medium from Jamaica, that there was someone around me that was carrying negative energy that needed to be cleared. During training there would be several people who opened up at different levels. There would be a big elevation of energy during one of the first meditations of the training. One student would have a spontaneous awakening that would last for a week. She would come into a place that needed to receive compassion and allow her to move through in her own time. After the training, I would need to bounce back and clear my energy. I started to understand and put forth the time necessary, to take care of and heal myself, in order to hold the space in helping others heal. This clearing would give me more space to see where people would go and allow me to support people who were moving through things that were unknown to most.

The fourth transformation that came to me in the form of pain showed up when I was leading a training outside of my home studio. I was in the midst of witnessing how the studio owner was moving from a place that was not aligned with what we were standing for. It got to a point where I had to make a stance for me. As we moved through the week, I would come into the realization that I would have to hold my space, that if I was going to live out my mission, I would have to allow some people to move forward in their way. I would learn how to stand for myself in the name of love, in every way.

I would once again be knocked down from this training. I would land in bed for a shorter period of time. I knew to rest and give myself space to bring forward balance in a bigger fashion. At this point in time, it was time to recognize me and be willing to lift myself up. In order for me to be there for others, I must first take care of me, and to complete my mission, I may have to walk away from one to reach the world. This was the fourth stage, and I knew deep within I was ready to move forward for all.

I paint because it gives me the space to listen deep within, with no true destination, just pulling out what is within to create a new picture. I am watching because it is time to paint a new masterpiece. For the last seven years, I've had the pleasure of raising my boys and moving through life with them as a unit. My daughter lives with their mom, and both have been a part of our lives as well. I realized as my son Trent began to pack his bag today, that in just over a month, he would be on to his next adventure. I built a yoga studio that allowed me to have my kids around all the time. It allowed me to have lunch with my son every day and the freedom to sit down with my family for dinner at night. It allowed me to provide for my kids and do what I loved to do, which was and still is, teaching the masses. It has also allowed me to pass the torch onto my oldest son, Sid IV, so he can live what he has been part of and known for most of his life. Now mind you, I have prepared both of my sons to get to this point, to leave the nest and spread their wings, so they and the world can see them be the greatest success they could ever imagine. And yet, no one told me to prepare myself for what I feel now. No one told me that my heart would feel so hurt, and yet feel so full of joy. No one really explained that to love someone is to prepare them and set them free, or that putting all of me into my kids would hit me like this. I feel overwhelmed as I sit back and start to paint this new picture.

As I prepare to take my son away to college, I too am preparing for another adventure of my own. It has been a true blessing to see my children grow their wings, and our connection will never fade as I step back and allow them to find their way. As they begin to take flight, I remember it is time for me to fly again as well, to live my mission and fill the hearts of many. I am preparing to travel the country for a year and see what's next as I spread my wings and reach for a new span of my own. I am ready to spread peace to every corner of our country and the world. Time moves along so fast. Embrace each moment, and let them flow in and out. Take a moment, stop and smell the roses, hug your kids, and let them know you love them. Share everything about yourself, even the parts you judge yourself for. I have always wanted to empower my kids to stand up and be the best that is possible in them, even if it meant against me. I am extremely proud to know that who I call my best of friends,

I also call my kids. We have begun anew, and I am happy through and through.

We all will find our way on the journey. Everyone is walking the same path, we are born, and then we leave this life. In between, we get to choose the turns we will take, yet we are still moving through the journey. Everyone will come to learn to live a life of love for one another. It is important to understand that we are all playing a game, and within the game, it is about having fun while in the midst of the game. I have moved through several stages and it is now time to awaken the warrior within all who are called to open up. I was blessed to get to lead Warrior Quest and to see the many different outcomes. The steps along this path are truly a sight to see. There are many different ways people come into their journey. Some need the space to move along the path in their way, and this may mean parting ways for part of our journey, as the space opens for all involved.

Leading Warrior Quest, and standing for others was again another level to my mission. I see how just the mere desire to want to quest for your soul's calling will cause an energetic shift, a time to begin an ignition in your body that will cause you to spontaneously move forward along your journey. You will walk further on the path and heighten your energy within. What is it you want in your life? What are you committed to doing? Right here, right now, this is why we have connected, so that you, too, can find peace in your heart and be exactly what you came here to be. It is truly your soul's calling. What you have been seeking is calling to you all along. When we sit by the tree of life together, it will not make a difference from where you came. It doesn't matter if you came and just needed to learn to finish a project. It doesn't matter if you are facing the journey of your life's creations. It doesn't matter if your mind is scattered. It doesn't matter if you are closed to the process or open to it. The Warrior's Quest is a course you will take when it calls you from deep within.

I have many people in my life. I stay with those who are willing to stand, and many of us have been a stand for each other for many years. When you are ready to stand for your friends, your family, your community, your nation, and the world, you will plant your feet and stand. It takes a warrior to stand strong because they have rid themselves of fear and are truly able to stand in peace for all. This is the Nahi Warrior Way, and those who live in this way are my brothers and sisters.

Many moments have passed, and it seems the foundation that was established from the very beginning, has brought me to land in Spirit. As I look around, I notice that "Spirit" is missing for many. It is from the game of life and the lessons from relationships and circumstances I have met along the way that parallel the many lessons on the field, that now allow me to bring forward a new teaching titled, "The Spirit of the Game." In the pages of the "Spirit of the Game" you will take a journey into the sports world as a guide that will help you in the healing of our world. As seen in the lessons of the game of life, connections to becoming more than others expect of you and reaching your fullest potential are all major parts gained in a team atmosphere. Many of these lessons are the lessons people are looking for in the day-to-day moments. It is through the pages of this book that you are given an opportunity to embrace the spirit of the game, allow it to resonate, be put into practice in your life, and begin to expand your world into a world full of peace, love, and abundance.

As you continue to read this book, know that the lessons and moments I share are coming forward from the interaction with many coaches, team-mates, and inspirations of family, fans, and players that have been part of this amazing walk with me. Thank you for taking the time to read this book. May you find that you have been inspired to reach deeper within and discover the life you are meant to live. For those of you I have yet to meet, and those I have shared space with, I thank you. I am grateful to be able to share with you "The Spirit of the Game."

I coached in three cities, moving across state lines three times in a year and a half. It was tough leaving friends and players you connected with and developed brotherly love and deep friendships with. I remember leaving my first job, and being reluctant to do so. Bob Spoo was a father to me in coaching. He taught me so much, as he did all of his coaches, but it was my dear friend, Randy Melvin who said it was okay to move on. We had a saying in coaching: "Until our eyes meet again," meaning there is never goodbye, as we knew that one day we would cross paths again. I've been very fortunate to see Randy, even though we never lived again in the same state. So until our eyes meet again, enjoy life. Stay golden, and live well. Now is your time, your time to get up and get off the bench. The Spirit of the Game is written to help you play the game to its fullest. Ultimately we are reaching to play the game of life with great ease, love, and joy. The principles within this book have been shared to help lift you down your path and live the best life you are able to live in this moment. Enjoy every breath and stay open.

PART TWO

SPIRIT OF THE GAME AND THE GAME IS LIFE

There Is Only One Law in the Universe: Everything Will Change

This is a story of forgiveness. While the details of my life appear different, it is the same spiritual story told since the beginning of time. In writing this down, I seek to prove that everyone can become their own yogi.

For most of my life, I thought I had to do something. Like many people, I thought I had "to do" because I wasn't acceptable and needed to prove myself. It took me over thirty years to learn how wrong I was and to see that what I needed was right in front of me. In order to achieve my goals, I didn't need to add more trophies, women, or cars. There was no status that would have satisfied me. In order to reach peace, I had to stop, breathe, listen, and BE. It is this aspect of "being" which is the most natural thing for us, but also the most difficult. It's not enough to just "know" the truth, or even to "do" the truth. We must BE the truth, and then all of our actions, words, and thoughts will naturally shine with the light of God. This is my living testament of walking with this God-like truth that I call love. All spiritual stories travel along a similar arc: from fear to love, from darkness to light, from turmoil to peace, from separation to God. In this book, there are many stories. I know now that each setback was a discovery, each bruise was a gift, and each blame was a lesson. It has led me to this point in my life where I have nothing but forgiveness.

My time as a football player and coach has become a guiding force in my life. Sports and coaching gave me the discipline and philosophical understanding of how to change. The lessons I learned on and off the field have served me very well as I continue to explore my spirituality and wellness. The lessons I have learned on the yoga mat have also helped me immensely. I know that, ultimately, there is no difference between great coaches, players, yoga followers, and spiritual practitioners. We are all one in our drive to become better.

I am a yogi, and so are you. The only difference between me and the average person is that I know what I am naturally, and I see many reject their own knowing. In the rejection comes discomfort and anxiety, and then they start the cycle of trying to "do" in order to relieve a deep subconscious pain. But this pain originates in doubt. If there was no doubt, then there would be no anxiety, no pressure, and no fear. If each person lived without doubt about who they are naturally, there could never be another argument, another divorce, another war. There would only be love and understanding. That is the true purpose of yoga and prayer. To reinterpret Shakespeare's "Hamlet," the question isn't "to be or not to be" but rather, what is the choice we make in life? We will always "be" something either out of love or out of fear. The choice is "to forgive or not to forgive." In the case of the famed brooding man, Hamlet could not forgive, and so he died. That is the definition of tragedy. In the case of Jesus, Lord Buddha, Krishna, Abraham, and many others, they chose forgiveness, and so they did not have to die. That is the definition of salvation.

In this book, you will find my story and my lessons flow in the same stream. I have taken time to separate out particular phrases throughout the chapters that can be repeated throughout the day. These phrases aren't ancient gospel, but simple clear statements set in the present and first-person. You can say them aloud, in your car, in crisis, or in prayer. The goal is to awaken your own inner voice and yogi. You don't need to believe in me or my story to gain benefit from these thought mantras. You don't even need to believe in yourself. You just have to be open to your own potential for something greater.

"I trust in a higher power; therefore all is possible."

The peace of God is my peace within. There is nothing else. When we are in a deep state of peace, a light shines forth and joins with others. May the light touch you and your world. It is my hope as you read these stories, you find your forgiveness, and Be Love.

*Best parents I could have
asked for in this life.*

*Happy days in
Baton Rouge, La.
June 26, 1970.*

*Four years
old and
having fun
with life,
post eggs.*

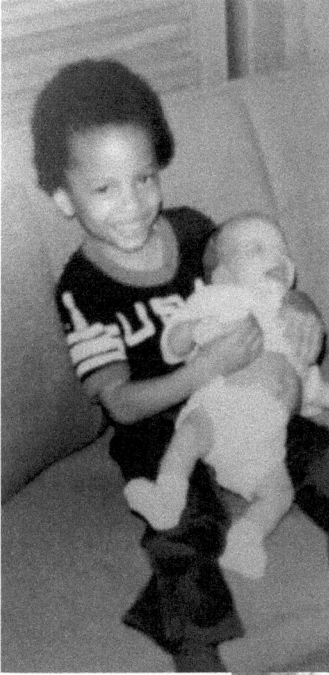

Loving having my brother David, my new playmate.

King and Prince of Mardi Gras.

In elementary school at Stedwick Elementary in
Montgomery Village, MD.

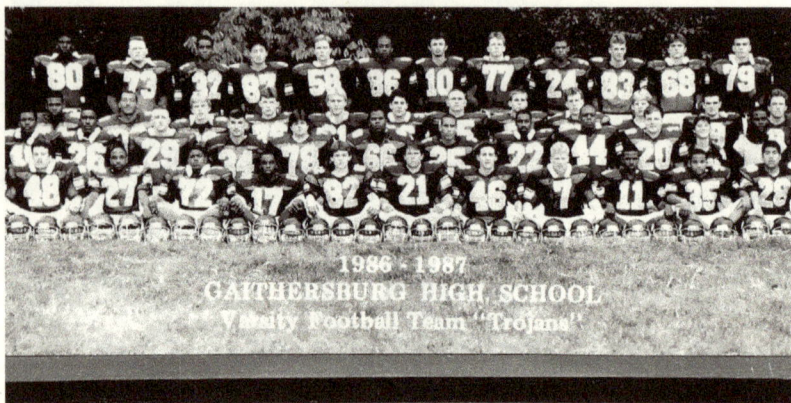

1986 - 1987
GAITHERSBURG HIGH SCHOOL
Varsity Football Team "Trojans"

| 1986 | GAITHERSBURG HIGH SCHOOL "Trojans" MARYLAND STATE AA CHAMPIONS LEAGUE RECORD: 9 - 1 OVERALL RECORD: 12 - 1 | 1987 |

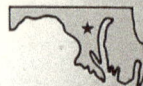

High School Football 1986 State Champions.
Bottom Right #35.

Gearing up for the Mr. Gaithersburg contest.

Love the football faces, born to play.

Warriors! The best receiving corps and men I had the pleasure to be with.

Top Row: (Lt) Michael Archie, Justin McCareins, Darrell Hill, Keith Perry, David McDermott

Bottom Row: Turner Pugh, PJ Fleck, Sid McNairy, Kandras Bledsoe, Rob Lee

Camille was set to be a cheerleader from the very beginning.

Sid and TD, best of friends from the very beginning.

Last year coaching football at Morgan State University. First winning season in 24 years.

The light shined a little brighter after vision quest.

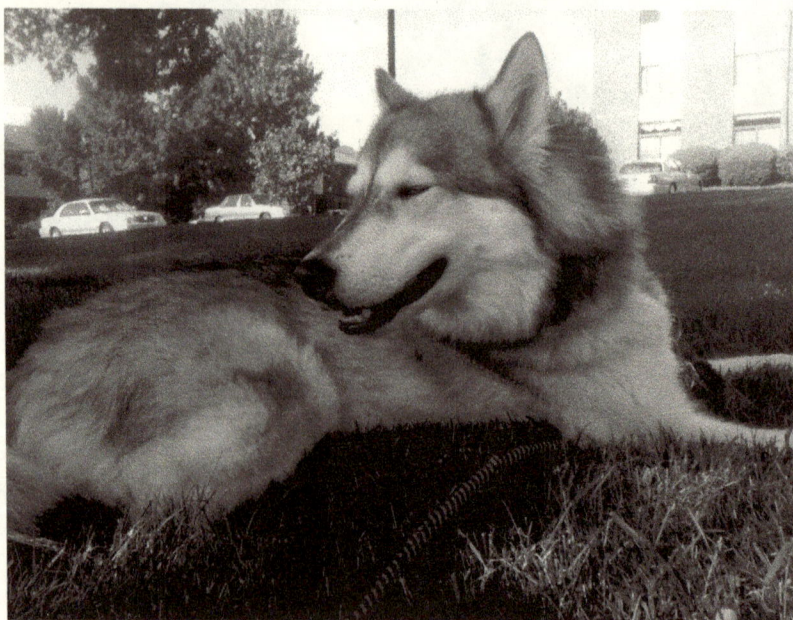

Our pet wolf, Shiva. Great teacher all around.

Coaching TD on the sidelines after he moved in with Sid IV and me.

After vision quest, Grandmother Morning Star was a guest on Conversations with Sid.

Beach time with family. We have a great life.

Vacations are fun at any age.

Getting ready to celebrate. Kids were happy I left coaching because they knew they would see me more.

Shift you and impact your community. Community Evolution.

Teaching at the Easter Egg Roll at the White House with President Barack Obama and Mrs. Michelle Obama.

Handstands with Baron Baptiste. Fun, fun times.

*Running into my man MC Yogi at Wanderlust Festival.
Love teaching and hanging with friends.*

*Sid getting ready to play for coach PJ Fleck at Western
Michigan University.*

Happy birthday to the best mom and mimi around.

After my hypnosis, Liz and I are visited by dolphins often.

"Walk with Love," music inspired by love and new life to come.

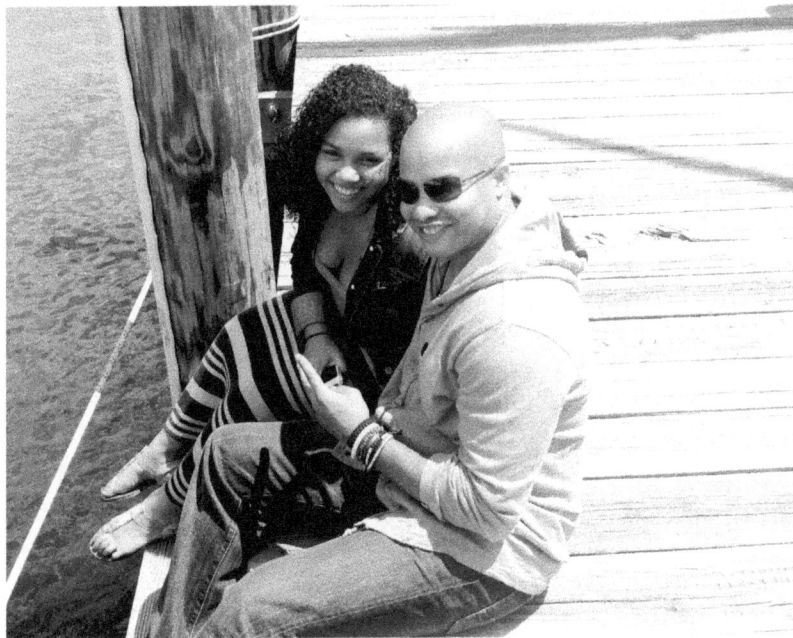

At the "Walk with Love" video shoot, between takes.

Love getting into the groove with Krishna Das "KD."

The eagle nation, my spirit in every way.

When we run into each other unplanned. Seeing Rick in Naples, friends for life.

Happy birthday to me. Hanging with my dad, good good times.

Getting recharged with yoga by the stream.

Krigsman Yoga, the first seed studio in Hingham, Massachusetts.

Preparing for our first concert. "Nahi" great times and awesome music with friends and family.

First concert for Nahi.

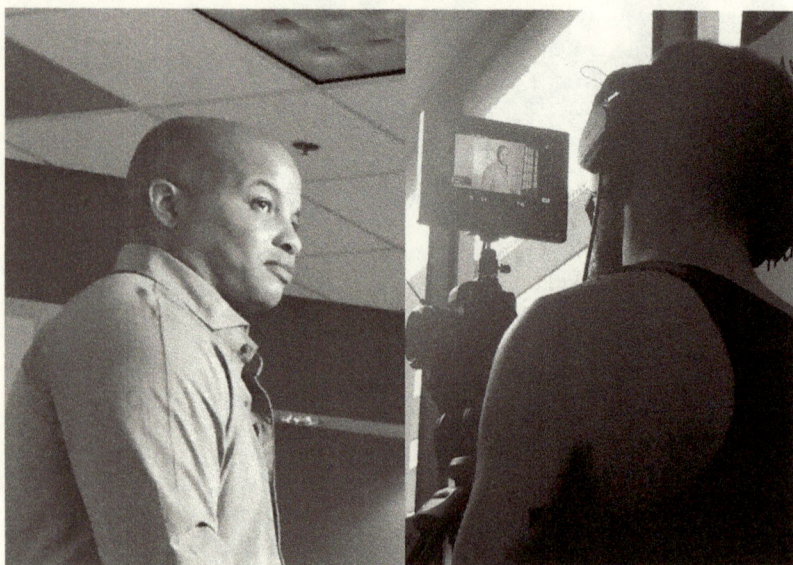

Staying wth the times. Teaching on a new medium,
UDEMY, "Yoga and Life Empowerment."

Love catching this shot of #LovelyLiz in California.

*Mentor and Spiritual leader for Poly Technical Institute
with Coach Sam Brand. Maryland State Champions.
2017*

*Passing the studio on to Sid IV. A studio built by warriors,
for Warriors.*

It is our yoga practice that gives us the ability to sit with what is.

Moving full circle, finding a way to be in meditation.

"Nahi Warrior" is one who is powerful and ready to stand in peace for the world.

CHAPTER 1
Sports and Spirit

Often for an athlete or a team to gain access to spirit, the experiences must be different. The doors must be opened in order to find a way into another level and a deeper connection to coming into the flow.

Sports have been part of my life as long as I can remember. It is through many sports analogies that I can truly reflect on my life. I was usually involved with team sports, so through that design, I have been able to look at my life and bring back the spirit that resides deep inside my soul. My family has helped in shaping many of my operating strategies that have molded the way that I have approached life. If you have made it this far, well done. Please know that you can release the need to hope, or try to reach for a new you. You are perfectly planted here, with all the tools that you need, to progress in a powerful, fun, and loving way. If you are living a human life, you are where you are and no need to change. You can now transform and open up to living this life from a sense of being empowered, moving beyond your wildest dreams.

There are several codes of conduct that come up, and as you move through gaining an understanding of these codes, you will begin to shift your way of being. In that shift, you will begin to see how your life begins to transform as well.

"Because I am Human I am Perfect!"

The first code of conduct is FAMILY – Forget About Me I Love You, implemented by PJ Fleck, Head Coach of University of Minnesota. While I was coaching, I can remember being a little different. I used to live life from a space of "me, me, me" as opposed to "team," even though we preached team. Regardless of me pulling many things together for the benefit of our team to learning to win, I still did a lot of things from a me perspective. What was it going to do for me? How was it going to help me? How was I going to advance in my career?

It's kind of like the fear we live through in everyday life. It's like when you go to college, you go to get the right degree. You get the right degree to get the right job. You get the right job, you'll end up with the right spouse. You get the right spouse, you'll have the nice beautiful house. If you have the nice house, you'll end up with the great car, and eventually, have great kids. That's the only way you can live your life in a fulfilling way in the system that we live in. So I began to challenge that, to begin to understand the meaning of, "Forget About Me, I Love You."

In learning that acronym F.A.M.I.L.Y., I saw how I could not only help myself, but how I could help everyone around me learn to live it in every way. This was a profound realization that came when I began to shift my mode of operation and my way of conduct as a coach. I learned about where I was and how I was standing. I noticed that I had a really great talk. Our team, as many teams do, would always talk about God first, family second, and then team. Yet, when it came down to it, we often would end up putting team first. We spent more time on the road and more time staying in the office, being without our families, just to get the win, and ultimately, sacrificed our relationships with each other as well, as a result of it.

As I said, in the beginning, my goals were generally about advancing my career, as opposed to figuring out how to be happy in life. When I was able to begin to shift that, I began to see how they really went hand in hand. My happiness triggered the success in my life. As I became more family oriented, new direction became possible. Four of my players would become my daughter's godfathers. PJ Fleck, Justin McCareins, Darryl Hill, and Deon Mitchell, also went on to play in the NFL. Our relationship developed into caring about one another on a deeper level. We formed a brotherhood that invited them into my home to get to know my kids and the life we were living. It was more than just what we were doing on the field that was going to make us winners. We came together as a true family, and as I shifted and eventually moved on from coaching, we remained in contact for many years to come.

My son went on to play college football at Western Michigan, for coach PJ Fleck, who was the head coach there before becoming the head coach of University of Minnesota. I would discover that he adapted the F.A.M.I.L.Y. concept in his coaching as a way to shift and motivate the team as well. I was very grateful to continue to have this relationship with my player, and have him be able to help my son, and figure out where his opportunities lay. I know it benefited my son having the support of someone who's been part of his tribe.

We've often been told that no single person raises another. A chief isn't born a chief. It takes a tribe to raise a chief, to build a strong person that can stand for the tribe. To build a big-time player, it takes more than just his one person. It takes a head coach, a position coach, a coordinator, pretty much everyone coming together to make sure that that person gains access and understanding to everything about them. Family also relates to creating community around you, where we are together and able to grow and lift each other up. Even after my son went to play at Western Michigan, it's the love that he had that supported him to leave football and be able to teach yoga

full-time. Him finding his own path, and his heart truly opening up through the love that was embraced and the freedom to
continue to grow, brought him to become an excellent teacher
today and fulfills him in helping people, even football players,
open up to their lives as well.

"My Future Is Righteous." -Bob Marley

In my life, the shifts have taken place for me to have space to
begin being one for all. When we allow this to open up, we
begin to see how we can all embrace giving and growing in
the factors beyond where we are today. Once we begin moving through the opening spaces of how we are able to flow
through life, we then begin to circle back, and as we move
full circle, we start to move into a new phase of standing and
helping others.

It is interesting to see that as I experienced all of the false
steps, I would find myself heading in the desired direction. My
experience in my relationships would lead me through several
steps, in order to come back around to a place of desiring to
help those who are in the experience of relationship with themselves. We all have evolved from the first cell. The first cell
began to look at itself. Once it figured out what was not going
to elevate the next cell, it discarded what was not needed. After
that, it took what was left, and divided itself in two, and gave
of itself to the next generation. This ultimately, is what we are
at the core. It is up to each of us to share with another, let go
of what is not needed, take what we have learned, and pass it
along to others.

Rebuilding happens when we hit a moment of breakdown,
where we have made a commitment to ourselves or another,
and then miss the mark as we know it. We miss that mark by
failing in our commitment to ourselves to be love for another.
The only way to begin to rebuild, is to recommit. By recommit-
ting, we all can come out of the breakdown stage, and open
up to what is possible in our relationships and in our lives. We
often see this as a stage that a team experiences as well. They
lose and fall into the depths of a breakdown. Often a team stays
in the way of losing because they have missed on connecting to

the awareness that something can and must be shifted to move forward. The breakdown can continue to pull us down when we have missed the opportunity to rebuild. Those in power see it, and pull in the head coach for a meeting. He can then see this as an opportunity to create a new reality, or remain in a losing mode. Often, a new coach is hired, and a new commitment is established, at least at the upper level. Often the process starts over, and the same downward spiral continues. It is here, where the link of rebuilding must be connected. The coach must also recruit the players to firmly fall in line with the new commitment. When this is successful, you see the shifts land.

"We are one heartbeat away from a shift within."

The breakthroughs take place when everyone has bought into the new vision of the new head coach. The more people that we bring into the fold, the sooner transformation will take place. Remember, we are always one heartbeat away from a true shift within. What is it you truly want? Are you willing to shift your foundation so that you can stand in your new commitment?

I have been blessed to sit with people all over the world. I used to sit with them and be empathetic about their situation. I would come away feeling how this would set into my body. I would see a new way for them and ultimately, it would shift in that moment. They would have a breakthrough. The miss was that in time they would go back and fall right back into the same pattern. A breakdown was inevitable. I eventually learned that I had a vision that was not realized in their mind. I started getting to a point where I decided to recruit them into a commitment to their own life shifts. This was where the house was built solid and could stand the test of time as they were able to recommit and able to build anew for themselves.

The five building blocks to successfully building and re-building are: The Attitude of Gratitude, Learning to Celebrate Every Moment, the Pursuit of Greatness, Determination, Trust that Love Will Win in Every Moment, and the Heart of a Champion.

It is time for everyone to come of A.G.E.: Attraction. Gratitude. Execution.

We will do this by learning to attract, practice gratitude for all, and execute and live it at all times. The first part of coming to age is to grasp that we are all like magnets, pulling to us our heart's desire. What has come to be right now is that most have unconsciously brought into life a reality they never would have desired to live in. For example, a few athletes understand this, and those who do move forward and begin to go from competing as kids to high school athletes. There are few who are blessed with coaches who know the art of creating, and can help them reach their potential at any given moment. For those that do advance into being college athletes, the process takes place again, but the stakes are now higher. Some work at grasping this in their own way, to be able to excel in every way. The numbers decrease, over and over, until the elite are left competing for their ability to get to a place where others only dream of.

Get ready, because you are not just anyone. You came here for a reason, you have and can know that reason within to go, and be exactly what the world is calling for. You created this world from the inside out. This is a possibility for all, and it starts with you beginning to bring into your life what you truly desire. It is a choice to make a shift. Know that you are in the flow always. As you become more aware of it, you will call forward what you are seeking. You are attracting to you what you are strengthening as a higher calling. It is up to you to allow this shift to happen. The couple who is living in strife is lost in pulling forward struggling moments. The team that continues in its losing ways has been practicing losing over and over. It is up to you, and every individual, to allow the shift to take place.

Practice. Practice. Practice. Gratitude will begin to generate and strengthen what you are bringing into your life. The more you express your gratitude, and the more moments you connect to the flow, the more you will be open to creating the shift. While I was in coaching, I spent countless nights preparing for the next game or looking at how I could prepare for the next job. While forgetting to smell the roses where I was, it was a big lesson to open up and see that I had a life, and many moments that I loved. It is the awakening of gratitude that allows us to access the flow of what we desire and to cultivate the reality we wish to see.

In the coming of AGE principle, it is a commitment to practicing and executing. Execution is when you are completely in the flow and continuously moving with grace and ease, ultimately coming into the alignment of the unconscious and pure flow of spirit.

As you read through "The Spirit of the Game," and the game is life, you will begin to see and understand the parallels between how a losing team performs on the field and the setbacks we have in life, as well as teams who have gone on to become champions, paralleling those who are achieving and reaching that space of manifesting their desires successfully in an easy manner. The loser's mentality comes from a specific place, and in that place, there is generally a miss on reality, a story that has been created that plays over and over in their head. That story then echoes into their body, a sensation we then label as a feeling of some sort. From that feeling, there is a vibration that begins to go out into the world. That vibration begins to attract a reality, like a magnet drawing into their life whatever they have thought about.

It has been stated that your thoughts are actually worse than your actions. The reason for that is that your thoughts come first, and your thoughts are creating the reality, creating what you're attracting, and what you're being ruled by, which often comes from uncontrolled, unconscious thoughts of the mind. So as you read on, you'll start to see more of the parallels of how your life resembles the actions of a winner or a loser. I want you to go beyond just winning or losing at life. To begin, you must understand and recognize that everything is good in your life. It's all always good, and in this moment, as well as every moment, you have an opportunity to realize what is good about everything. From the infinite source of nothing, all things will be born.

"My gratitude lifts up my life."

The Attitude of Gratitude takes practice. It is an art, an art of seeing the greatness in all moments. It has been seen in sports through tragic moments, moments when a player may be injured, or the tragedy of death itself. We perceive when a coach is penalized for standing up for his players as a tragic moment. The moments often show up as a spiritual breakdown. Through looking at and examining this breakdown, we can reconnect, and rebuild. To find the best in these moments is how we can lift up to new heights.

I had a chance to witness my son Trent have a major moment take place in his football career. He became the first starting freshman quarterback at his high school. Questions came up before the start of his first game. Should he start? Is he ready? He went on to start against Perry Hall, a team that went on to the playoffs. Because of my coaching years prior, and then being the offensive coordinator, the special teams coordinator, and the assistant head coach for TD's high school his freshman year, there were many oppositions to this decision.

We had a junior as our starting quarterback who was sent out of our second game of the season with a concussion. All the coaches had watched and worked towards building TD's confidence. We watched as he began to flourish. He had a great week of preparation before our third game and went into the game ready and set to lead his team. We found ourselves down in many ways, as he seemed to be running for his life. The players in front of him were outmanned. The opposing defense had their ears pinned back and were running free. Despite it all, TD stepped up and completed a few passes, and was willing to stand in it, and dig in deep. In the second quarter, we called a sprint out pass that called for him to get outside and have an option to run, or pass. Two guys were free, and he was sacked. As he hit the ground, his helmet caught his jaw and broke his jaw.

Here we were, several breakdowns. The breakdown for TD was how, at fifteen, he would respond to a moment most never experience. While on the field, he threw his helmet off, told the trainers and the head coach to let him up. "I need to get up for my team," he said. Lesson number one.

He then came to the bench. When I looked into his mouth, you could see the inward curve of his jaw. He kept saying it felt off. He reached in, and pulled his jaw, resetting his own jaw into place. Lesson number two.

He stood up when it was time for him to go to the hospital and leaned on my shoulder. I asked, "What, does it hurt that bad?"

He said, "No, it is my heart. I am hurting for letting my team down." Lesson Three.

He went to the hospital and when I arrived after the game, he was in great spirits. I wanted to let him know that I would support him and love him however that looked. I explained how proud of him I was, and I asked if he wanted to stop playing football. His reply was on point as he watched the NFL game on TV from his stretcher. "Well," he said, "it would be crazy for me to stop now." Lesson Number Four.

He chose to continue to play in life, as it has truly begun when you allow yourself to be in the awe of it. The practices shifted for him, as the attitude of gratitude had inspired him to jump in fully to a commitment that most never find. At fifteen years of age, he was challenged to evolve to a new place, from a breakdown, to major breakthroughs in so many ways.

His grades in school had continued to be exceptional because, wanting to play at a new school, Loyola Academy, run by Jesuits, he had to excel in order to get in. He became a gym rat, spending up to six hours in the weight room at a time, not because he was asked but because he desired to get bigger to protect himself and grow as a player. He learned how to lead and when it was time to speak up, as well as when it was time to just listen on a deeper level and let others lead. Having his jaw wired shut, he had no choice, but to learn how to listen. Coming away from all of this enabled him, beyond a shadow of doubt, to see just where and what he desired to reach for in his own life, something many never find, and some much later in their lives. He learned many lessons from the setback, only to go on to excel in such a powerful way.

Learning to celebrate every moment is a complement to an attitude of gratitude. For when we learn to celebrate, we take the time to not only acknowledge and appreciate, but to actually learn how to rejoice—rejoice in the lessons that come from the moments that we used to dub as "bad," showing the universe we are happy for the moments that come our way. The more we can strengthen that vibration, the vibration of celebration, the more we will attract the things that we want. So learning to celebrate is to actually find victory, even in the moments of defeat.

I remember when I was coaching at Northern Illinois University, we were one of those staffs hired to take over a program that had been losing. When we won our first game to break our streak, our players learned to celebrate. They rejoiced in the moment so much that they attracted space to open up new doors of possibility. They saw that if they kept winning, they actually had a chance of going from losers to opening up the door to being a winner, over and over, to shifting the energy internally and collectively to open up to a new space.

So learn to celebrate in your life the moments of defeat as well as the moments of victory, to begin to see how you can open up to a deeper place within, that shifts your reality. Celebration delivers something new. Learn to see the flower sitting in the field and celebrate the miracle of how it came to be. Learn to see the birth of a baby and celebrate how it came to be. Learn to see your life each day as a miracle, like the miracle of the sun rising. Celebrate and understand the miracle of the passing day gone. Celebrate all of the moments that have come your way. Celebrate until your heart sings for the pure joy of each day that has come.

I coached quite a few different sports in my lifetime, and I remember early on, when my players would rejoice in scoring a touchdown or making a shot in basketball or scoring a goal in soccer, how they would celebrate less and less in the season. In sports, you find that when you celebrate the small victories, you start to understand that defeats are only opportunities to learn how to succeed. I challenge you in this way, to open up to celebrating more and receiving the gift of seeing things from a new viewpoint.

"Today I live in my greatness."

The pursuit of greatness takes time to develop. You take the time by sitting back and giving yourself space to understand where it is you wish to be, to understand what it is you desire to bring forward, and allow your thoughts to mirror this. You take the time to set goals to see what it is that you want and how you can begin to bring it forward. With my players in college, when they first came as freshmen, I would sit with them and map out four or five years down the road with them, depending on if they were going to redshirt or not, meaning they sit out their first year. We would set goals for what they wanted their lives to look like at the end of the determined term. Some of them desired to be married in five years, others desired to play in the NFL, and fortunately, most of them desired to graduate. Then we went back and looked at what the first step would look like for them. For some, it was the understanding of just starting to play on the team. For others, it began to be the understanding of what it would look like to be a starter. In the case of our receivers, it looked like how many passes they might catch in their first or second year. For all, it was what their grades looked like to continue playing. In their third year, it was what it looked like as they began to draw the attention of the NFL. In their fourth year, it was to become an "All American," academically as well as on the field. And again for all, what it would look like to have graduated. All of this would be assessed so they could let go of the need to pursue anything but where they wanted to be.

This is what I challenge you to do. Sit down, and take the time to understand where you want to take yourself in the future. Then ask yourself how you can allow yourself space, in this moment, to create a reality that brings what you wish to be now, and beyond, giving yourself space to say, "Okay, where can I stretch myself? Where can I get outside of my normal paradigm and reach for something grander, reach to be something a little different?"

Usually we are living in a box, and that box becomes our paradigm. The paradigm or space of knowing where we are allows us to start to understand the possibility of being stuck in that box. From here we can stretch ourselves to go beyond our normal paradigm. At first, moving towards the unknown, you are going to go through what we call the fear barrier. That fear barrier is just a feeling that something is changing. So when you begin to let go of the need to label fear as a bad thing and watch things shift from the inside out, all things are possible. Find examples, examples in the world of what you wish to create in your life. For the most part, everything has been done before. So be willing to look around to see how others have lived before you, to see the example that can allow you to pursue greatness in your way. Maybe that example for you is God. Maybe that example is Buddha or Jesus. What is the example you can look at in your life, in the reality as you know it, to find the greatness that lies inside of yourself? There is a warrior waiting inside of your own heart. Are you willing to look and open up? Can you see where you are? The Olympian aspires for gold medals, aspires to break records, aspires to reach the greatest level possible within them. Be willing to aspire to be your greatest. To open up to what you can pursue for yourself that will set you free. Shoot for the moon, and if you miss, you'll land upon the stars.

And that is kind of how I approach my life. To go for it all and what if I did miss, would I be content with where I would fall? Usually the answer is yes. And through contentment I am able to open up the space beyond where I may have dreamed before.

"My victories in life are through my determination."

We used to have a saying on our offensive football team that we wanted our players to be physical and no excuses. To be physical and no excuses for us meant that no matter what we did, we were going to be physical. So if we came off the ball early, jumped off-sides, we wanted to be physical. If we came off the field and we lost, we wanted to be physical. If we came away from anything, we wanted to be physical and we were going to make no excuses and reach for it all – be physical, no excuses, and get it done! In the end we wanted to make sure that we were getting the job done that we were pursuing greatness.

I like to think of it as being unreasonable, to do things beyond the reasons that we normally make. We normally have the reasons of why we won't be able to do something. I couldn't get on time for work day after day because I caught the train crossing the road. I couldn't make my way to the dentist because I had something else to do. I couldn't spend my time with my kids because I had to work. So allow yourself space to understand how to be *unreasonable*. To go beyond making the reasons that hold you back in your life. Go beyond the reasons that we use for peer pressure to hold us back. Go beyond the reasons that we use to say that things are unsuccessful in life. Go beyond the reasons for why your relationships don't work. Be unreasonable in your life.

Walter Payton had a saying, "The game is 80 percent mental and 20 percent physical." The same can be said for life. Eighty percent of the things that will happen around you have come from the thoughts that you've attracted into your life. Twenty percent of them will be the things that you've just opened up to, because that's the way it is. So allow yourself space to understand where your physical and your mental makeup is coming from. How mentally you are attracting the reality, you are manifesting your reality consciously or unconsciously. Understand how everything is opening up for you. Through determination we will be able to see beyond, beyond where we are now. To pursue all of the things that can open up for you. So find determination in your walk.

"Today I am free of reasons to fail."

A champion goes for it all no matter what, not just the pursuit. A champion sees exactly where they are in every moment, because a champion has the determination to be a champion. Because it is deep inside their own heart, and the foundation that they come from, the foundation of where they live, and understanding is built solid from a strong space that's unshakable, even in the midst of a loss.

The definition of a champion is a person who has defeated or surpassed all rivals in a competition. In the competition of life, the champion of life, and the heart of a champion, comes from those moments when a person has decided to defeat their own fears, to continue to move forward beyond them, and to gain access to the heart, that space where love resides. Be the champion of all of your fears. See them to understand and to open up to being the witness to how you're living your life, going further than anyone may believe that you possibly could. Know that you are worth it, and worthy, to put it all into place. Reach for your greatness, whatever that looks like for you. You may want to be the champion father or mother, the champion sister or brother, the champion community leader or the champion president. Are you willing to put in the work to be the champion that you know is inside of you?

Know that no one is stopping you, except for you. There is no stopping; you pursue and persevere until you reach it. Whatever it is for you, pursue it in every way. The hunger within feeds you in every breath to reach within to see you were born to be a champion. Deep within you, the champion makeup is there. Open up to that mindset. Open up to knowing inside of you. It is the same makeup that is inside another. Have you realized you are a champion?

I recall one year, pursuing a winning season, our players had committed to a perspective of thinking that because they'd worn black socks and won some home games, that not wearing the black socks at our next away game meant they weren't sure that they could produce a win. I remember our head coach deciding to wear black socks for the benefit of the team's mindset, and told them to go be great anyway. They were able to shift their mindset, identifying what was real versus perspective, and were able to win the game. Are you willing to see beyond the outward circumstance? Can you find the mindset that opens up from your heart center to allow you to pursue your greatness? No one can do it but you.

A champion knows they've been there and trust that they will be there again. Begin to understand that in your own life, to understand that you can celebrate your successes because you've been there before. You understand them and have no need to be attached to them because you know they're coming back around. It's the same as an athlete, you know the great ones, they just keep scoring because they have been there before. Do the work, and see where the work will land you. Walk like a champion and begin to take the steps of seeing yourself walking in your own greatness. Talk like a champion. There is a talk; use this language to evolve deeper in your greatness. Champions talk about winning, champions talk about reaching their destiny. Champions have a way about them that's undeniable. Find that champion talk inside of your own mind. Think like a champion. Act like a champion. Be a champion.

CHAPTER 2
The Power of Faith

Spirit is all around you. It is up to us to embrace each moment, and stay open. By the power of faith, one will gain access to seeing from the truth of all. We are all able to come into the flow and see that we can create and take ownership for how our reality has been shaped. By staying open to spirit, you will gain access to the overall picture. Begin to do something new, create a new culture, find your team, evaluate and shift your life into its highest good.

You will begin to see over time, your resistance to staying open. This resistance comes from the mind, the mind chatter that is based on past experiences. As noted before, this locks us into a disconnect from the depths of love, which lies in the connection to God in every way. Take time to connect to the overall picture for you and the spirit running through you as an outward expression. It desires to bring you forward.

Your heart's desire is an expression of what you want. This can be brought forward by first understanding what it is you want. Take the time to see what it is that you desire to live like in the future. Look out into the future, as far as you can see. This may not be one hundred years or this may be one hundred years, fifty, twenty, five, or ten years. Begin by putting this into a vision for you. How old will you be, who will be there, where will it be? Bring this forward with as much detail as you can.

Once you have brought this forward, take time to drop within. Use the master chemist to bring this all forward. The master chemist I refer to is faith. Yes, faith. And you have it, even if you have yet to acknowledge it or where it comes from. The definition of faith is "complete trust or confidence in someone or something." You may say, "Where do I have faith?" I am fortunate to have come into life, and at six years of age, I had bronchitis, and because of this ailment, my faith was tested. I remember when I went to college, I was told I had sports-induced asthma. So I was put on inhalers to allow me to control this experience. It was in this that my faith was lost. Faith was lost in my breath because I had been given the ability to control the outcome myself.

What happened next, was life changing. At this time in my life, I drank a few beers and partied hard, to say the least. This gave me a chance to be free. At one of our parties, I had run out of my inhaler, and I began to have breathing problems. It got so bad that an ambulance was called. When they came, I said, "If you can give me an inhaler, I will be okay." I saw it in the medical box, but they did not give it to me. I began to get worse. As we were going to the hospital, I was losing my breath more and more. As we approached the hospital, I heard the team state, "Be prepared, when we get in, he will have ten minutes to live."

Wow, in that moment, I gave in. I learned faith: faith that it was really out of my hands. Thank heavens for that lesson, as I have since let go of control and now am more free. The point to this is that you have faith, as most do. You breathe every day, and few worry about it until it is lost. Now is the time to allow this to be applied to the rest of your life. Do something new. Apply faith to the part of your life you have lost faith in.

I recall my first trip to Jamaica. It was there that I applied my knowledge and allowed spirit to guide me. I went to Jamaica with Liz, and had no plan. I was told it would be guided by spirit, that spirit was there in the breath. It was interesting; I was too busy traveling and living my dream to actually plan it out. Things happened in this first trip. Had I stayed in my old way, we would have hit wall after wall. I was invited to speak at an invocation that was directed to an amazing moment of breath consciousness. The audience was primarily made up of people who had been incarcerated. All of whom, at one point, were on death-row. I had spoken to groups in this way before, yet this time I had no fear, no judgment, just faith that what spirit would have me talk about was exactly what was meant to be. It went so well that the group of guys shared they received more in the first ten minutes than they had in thirty years.

Another time, I was speaking at a rehabilitation center and again with the men who had been incarcerated, later in the week. In the midst of this, doors flew open to progress my life in a beautiful way. We went to the places that only spirit would flow. I met with a music producer that had helped in holding space for the word to move through the airwaves and transform lives. We had landed in two places that brought forth yoga in Jamaica in a huge way. Most of all, love had been found, and it was, and is, within my own heart.

Another piece to the power of faith is to create a culture, whether you are part of a team, corporation, community, tribe, or religion. In order for spirit to continue to move through your life, you must land in a culture. Sitting in many meetings, I have seen how spirit works through people. Spirit moves from one to the next, through like moments, and like vibrations. On a team, we see that when all pieces move in one heartbeat, they create an inner peace and an inner flow.

For me, yoga is my way, yoga is my lifestyle, much like that of a Rastaman. It is a deep understanding that we are all joined. As we look within, everything is provided for you. In our culture of yoga and in the Nahi Warrior community, our way of being and lifestyle has allowed me to grow with everyone in my life. Through the development of this lifestyle, it was important to find those who were of like-mindedness. Those who wanted to walk in this way of peace know they are my true brothers and sisters. It is in the support to reach a common mission that the lifestyle and culture has spread to all corners of the world, connecting the dots back together.

What is it that you want your culture to represent? How would you like your lifestyle to be? How will it look to touch others? How will spirit move, to bring it all together?

It is in the discovery of the answers to these questions that we are able to turn losing football teams into winning teams and falling societies into thriving communities. But first, you must create a culture within yourself and live a lifestyle that moves you in the direction of peace, love, and community.

Once you have it within you, you will then see that others want it. You are a magnet and what you have, others will see. Find those that see you, that understand you. This team of people are the ones who you are seeking; it lies dormant inside of everyone. Understand what it is you are creating. As you start to dial deeper within yourself, you will start to find your tribe and connect to those who will stand with you. Let them all the way in, let them understand the lifestyle. Once you connect to others, your tribe will begin to spread. Lean on each other, so that they can call you out in the moments you may miss the mark. The definition of sin is to miss the mark. Now that you know what is possible, you are able to be free of your sins.

I recall when coaching my players, I wanted to create a culture, a way that my receivers could live life and reach their highest good. Early on, we recruited the top players to be the example to show others just how we were going to be. It was these players that made our unit. Once they fully came into the fold, I would buddy them up with the younger players. This way, they looked out for each other and strengthened their understanding of the culture we were living. This unit went on to be so strong that four went on to play at their best in college and to have their personal stints in the National Football League. They have found in the NFL that when one family member makes it into the league, it is easier for others because they know how to work, and what it takes. My initial players affected every player that came into the unit after them. This group was willing to go on and be the example for others.

So, if you still are questioning how it works, it has become a science for us in many ways. It is a new operating system for all. I left Northern Illinois in 2001, and fifteen years later, my son went on to play for PJ at Western Michigan University. The message shifted a bit, but the culture was still there. Because of this culture, they went on to have an undefeated season before coach Fleck left to coach in the Big Ten Conference, at the University of Minnesota.

Build it, and recruit those to support your culture. Remember as you are opening up to spirit, be willing to step back and evaluate and shift when needed. In football, there are several periods when evaluations take place. Whether it is evaluating the production of an individual player or the efficiency of the training room, it is all meant to reach a new level. Take the time periodically to look at the facts. When looking at the facts, step back, and move forward from an open heart and free spirit.

CHAPTER 3
Pitfalls of a Warrior

I have sat in observance of how players move, and the great ones have a way about them that speaks for itself. That "it" I speak of, when you discover it, everyone feels it and wants to be part of "it."Often players run into pitfalls when they think they are it; these pitfalls take over when players believe it is their greatness that gives them access to their abilities.

The pitfall that many get trapped in is that they get lost in comparison, as opposed to remaining competitive about the actual process that they are in. Those who get lost in the comparison with others ultimately never fall into their own personal greatness. This becomes a waste of energy. By reaching for being competitive, we move forward in reaching for our own personal greatness. The competitive athlete strives for the space to improve along the way, no matter where they currently are. The competitive individual has an eternal fire that is turned on at the mere thought of competing with another, or even with themselves.

Another pitfall of many athletes is negative self-talk. They forget about lifting their own spirit and building their own greatness. Negative self-talk begins to plant seeds that ultimately lead us to failure and distraction. We have been programmed; we run a series of programs in our brain that keep us in the patterns we are in. The other option is to experience our pure power by building on the greatness within. It is up to each of us to look inside and begin to make an agreement with all we want to bring forward. It is through our language that the patterns we live in are continually brought forward. Those who advanced in any aspect of life had challenges. In the midst of their challenges, they knew deep inside that they were able to continue to look within and discover greatness. It is faith that allows us to continuously speak to ourselves in a way that will lift us up. Faith is that which allows us to move forward no matter what the circumstances are at hand. As time passes, developing faith becomes a key to opening the doorway to speak from a place of greatness within our own hearts of communication.

The next level of pitfalls comes from comparison of the mental-midget mindset and the mental giants. The mental-midget mindset holds us in the space that continues to have us playing small with life. We are crippled in our mind and can continue to stay locked into the patterns of our past. We continue to live from the perspective of what has been. Even if we have had success in the past, the mental-midget mindset causes us to stay within the paradigm of what has been. By doing this, we will continue to bring forward the past.

When our mind operates from the operating system of a mental giant, we are set in motion towards achieving big success. The mental-giant operating system is guided by the facts, anchored in what is real, and is accepting of how flow moves us in the direction of our highest self. We step out of the old and get ready to meet the world as a yes for what is next. By choosing the mental giant operating system, we open up to making our way to that of great possibility. We are guided from the source of all that continually flows us forward with the sense of freedom in the world around us. From this place, we are presented with several doors to walk through. As a mental giant, we are no longer consumed by our past. We open up to embracing what choices will allow us to move freely towards what will lead us to our highest good. By operating from the space of a mental giant, we are free to grow in every way.

There is a space that often consumes warriors that affects the community and may destroy the tribe from the inside out. The "locker-room lawyer," the town gossip, takes everyone around and down a dark hole, whereas a team captain or leader lifts everyone up, even in moments that may have seemed to be a setback. The locker-room lawyers are consumed with back talk. Their conversations are generally centered around complaints, and because of these complaints, they have lived them for many years prior. The locker-room lawyer lives from a space we call the *earth-self*. Operating from this space is to be consumed with how they must defend themselves from attack of the next place where love may be lost. The locker-room lawyer continues to operate from a mental focus that is all about them. The locker-room lawyer's focus limits their growth and the growth of those around them. Through the eyes of the locker-room lawyer, everyone is against them in the end. The defensive posture is limiting and causes them to get ready for defense of all loved loss.

We can view those who have shifted into a *we* mentality as "Champion Warriors," those who stand for others and lift all up, to reach their highest self. The team captain understands the mission of everyone involved and recruits others for the greater good of all. The Champion Warrior operates in the moment, in evaluation and observation of what is taking place. It is the Champion Warrior that truly sees from the eyes of helping everyone reach their highest self. Our greatest leaders have stood for others in the grand moments and done the same in moments that are not so grand. May you find that you land in the way of the Champion Warrior, no matter what you are doing.

Here is an observation of where many people's performance levels come from. There are several people who fall apart under pressure. There are individuals who are strong when nothing is at stake, or what we call the *practice performers*. When their focus moves outside of themselves, everyone including them, raises the bar and lands in a stronger place as a player and a team. It is important to see that many of us can perform when nothing is on the line. What we fail to see is that there is always something on the line. This is your life—are you willing to watch as it all falls away?

The other level of performance would be characterized again, by the "Champion Warriors." The Champion Warrior understands that every moment they are involved with has an impact on the world as a whole. The Champion Warrior understands what is at stake with every decision they make. A Champion Warrior reaches deep within and trusts their intuition to make choices in the moment, knowing their choices will land them in their highest good. Once an individual is operating in this way for many moments, they eventually only know how to operate from this way of being.

Another pitfall that individuals fall into is the comparison of the front-runner versus the Champion Warrior willing to walk the path. Those who are front-runners often fall to challenges. It is easy to live well when all is going your way. When individuals are attached to the things going their way, they shine well, and then fall apart when things are stacked against them. In the end, we can move forward with the individuals that we can count on. The Champion Warriors walking the path stand in the midst of any challenge. Circumstances are far from what makes them great. Greatness is an all-the-time thing, and the Champion Warriors come through in any moment. We walk the path to greatness by moving through what many see as failure, only to see in the end what is possible. When walking the path, we see just how success comes from seeing our setbacks as building blocks for our future. I have often said the more people we surround ourselves with on the path, the foundation is set, and the success is on its way.

As we continue to look at the pitfalls of players, we can see that the fallback resembles characteristics that cause us to fall behind and keep us from success. The next one is the winner versus the Champion Warrior. A winner is an individual who puts it together for one moment, a game, or maybe even gets lucky for a season. Winners find a way to put it together one time. There is a commitment that is lost over time. The lack of commitment, the lack of discipline that is needed to pass through life's challenges, crumbles, and the winner eventually falls behind. Over time, the ones we see who build a dynasty are the Champion Warriors in the end. The first part is the commitment that is made to success, no matter what is thrown their way. A champion mentality is a go-forward, no-matter-what-it-takes mindset, to have the discipline to continue to walk the path and to see things through. They find a way to success no matter what is in front of them, on or off the field.

The final pitfall we will look at is the space of arrogance. Many individuals fall when they are full of themselves. They have over time proven to themselves that they are good at their trade. The downfall comes when they carry this on their shoulders. Others begin to gun for them, to bring them back to a grounded place. The arrogant individual may also be knocked off of their pedestal by the creator, to humble them, and start over.

The flip side of arrogance is humility. The Champion Warrior who has humility has found the utmost of confidence, as they are no longer in need of being boastful. The player with humility has the confidence to show up time and time again. The humility gives way to an unshakable confidence that continues to grow over time, trusting that there is a power greater than oneself lifting them up.

In the end, to allow ourselves the ability to escape from the pitfalls of the game of life, we must turn it all over to Great Spirit. The Great Spirit that created you, that created me, that created everything, the one that ultimately gave you the gift inside of your heart to live every day, no matter what you are doing. Whether you were playing a sport or playing with life, something has got you.

"God's Got Me!"

CHAPTER 4
A Warrior's Heart

The heart is the house of the source of our power. It is the heart of a Champion Warrior that gives way to mastering life to its fullest. Through the four cornerstones of life, one will open their heart to gain the full potential of all that is within reach of us. In order to move into this full power, it is imperative that we move beyond the space of fear and into the potential of the greatness of love and the power within. When we are filled by the desire to grow, we continue to step towards evolution. In the process of evolution, we will continue to grow and reach our highest.

When I was coaching, I had a player who came to camp. This kid possessed great hands; he would catch anything close to him. The problem was, he was slower than most players we taught in the receiver position. I remember our head coach coming in and asking if I thought I could get him to play. My answer was yes. What he had was desire. I knew that if I fueled that for him, there was nothing that was out of reach. When he finally came to join the team, we sat and went through goals, as I did with all of my players. He had a goal of being a starter by the time he left. I recall when we went through goals as a unit, his teammates were surprised to see him shoot for it all. In that moment, an NFL player was born. They were convinced he had it. Over the next four years, he would go on to set records at the school and go on to be an all-conference player. When the 49ers came to scout him, he ran the fastest he had ever run. It was the burning desire to grow in every way that continues to fuel him, even after being a player. He also had a goal of going back home and becoming his high school's head coach. His desires were grand. In that moment, when he announced his goal, I recall saying, "Going back to be your high school coach is great, but why your high school? You can go on to be a great college coach, or on to the NFL. Whatever you want, you can do it. Once he completed playing, he went on to coach. The desire burned bright, and at the age of thirty-one, he went on to be a Division-1 head football coach. The story is being written, I am proud to watch it all unfold as PJ Fleck goes on to be so much more than he initially dreamt of being.

The heart of a Champion Warrior can also be discovered in the midst of a challenge, a test that has shown up and caused a shift within, an opportunity to go in and lift to a place that is unknown in the current awareness. There are times when due to a level of perceived hurt or pain, one may land in a spiritual bankruptcy, and we must look within to find trust and faith in something greater to lift us up. When we hit these lows, we can let go, and trust in the support of all that is seen and unseen.

When we look around, does the tree yell when its branches are broken? Does the seed of the rose flower freak out when the world puts pressure on it to grow? You, too, can find ease in your perceived setbacks, and be open to the growth that comes along with reaching back and lifting off. When we enforce that the universe is evolving, and we are part of this expression in this way, we will be open to all growing moments to come.

The heart of a Champion Warrior is built in faith. The faith you were born with was God-given, and no one can take this away. When a Champion Warrior has moved into the faith phase of learning, he or she has come to understand deep within that all things will come to be in time. The heart of a Champion Warrior gives us an opportunity to connect to the highest. In this space, we are able to come into the full flow of oneness with all. The heart of a Champion Warrior understands that even his competition is one with his highest.

As a champion of life, we may find ourselves on the field ready to battle, ready to lift up, and it brings all of us out to play. When we sit back and land in our heart, we find gratitude for everyone involved. We understand that everyone in the game is there for each of us to reach our highest. When you sit back and look at the big picture, everyone involved in the world is one. One throws the pitch, one hits the ball, one fields the ball, one runs the bases, one throws the ball, one starts, and one stops. We are all in the same game—this game we call life. We are all in it, and it takes each of us to live it fully.

The core traits of a Champion Warrior come through over time, for every individual. It is through unconditional love for one's self and everyone else that each trait is birthed, and many others grow from within. From the practice of self-love, all of the strongest qualities will continue to rise up. In this time, it is important that we recognize there are set ways of being that align us to spirit and continually elevate us into a deeper state of love. The warrior who comes into the dance with spirit has traits that continually elevate them into their highest. By cultivating the Heart of a Warrior into your own life, you will find that you, too, will gain access to the flow and live the life you desire with support from all around.

The first trait to cultivate is having a sense of modesty. We are all created in the likeness of the infinite source. The source is the originator. When we give ourselves space to come into agreement with these characteristics, anything is possible of all things, and with this awareness, we can find a sense of modesty knowing that all things have been gifted to us. By allowing this to be accessed within ourselves, we gain the space to allow support to come forward and move us into the flow. When we land here, we are able to see and understand that all things are able to be created on our behalf.

There is an old story of a champion fighter named Goliath, and a shepherd boy named David. David was an Israelite, the son of an Ephrathite named Jesse, who was from Bethlehem, in Judah. Jesse had eight sons. The three oldest were said to follow the leader to war. There was a great Champion from the Philistines. His name was Goliath, and whenever Goliath would come out to the battlefield, all of the Israelites would leave in fear. Goliath was a large man, the biggest man ever seen, and most would tremble with fear around him. After long battles, David the shepherd boy found his way to the battlefield. He went to King Saul and said that he would go and defend their honor. Now, mind you, David was a shepherd boy, so he was small in comparison to most soldiers. Yet he had something different. He had heart. So when David went to the battlefield, everyone was worried that he would die. Not only did David have heart, he also fought with precision. He developed a sharp skill of using a sling with stones. This would propose an advantage over Goliath. He would be able to keep his distance and do whatever it took in order to win. Once they began to battle Goliath would throw his spear, and try to track David down, but David kept his distance until the opportunity presented itself. At this point, David was able to take a stone and launched it into Goliath's head. When the stone hit Goliath in the forehead, it did not come out. This gave the Israelites a new-found life, and they were able to defeat the Philistines.

David, like each and every one of us, had a desire. He had developed the discipline to execute what was needed, in order to champion his life that day. We can see through the story of David and Goliath that by David letting go and trusting in something greater, he was able to conquer the great Goliath, and he went on to open up to many amazing moments in his life. Through modesty, we also learn that others are willing to support us on our way forward. There is great ease in helping others when they are approachable and at ease with who they are in their own greatness.

Another trait we seek to land in is to gain a deeper connection and openness to spirit in one who is inspired. When we are inspired, we gain an open space to the spirit within. An individual who is inspired is filled with the urge to do or feel something creative or exemplary. Inspiration is reflected outside of ourselves in the people or circumstances outside of our body. But it is within our hearts that spirit will shine through. This inspiration shows up in our desires, what drives us to keep going, what lifts us up to our highest.

Ultimately, my inspiration is built around creating peace all over the world. So, no matter what it is I am doing, I am looking to create peace and a state of ease for all that allows us to continue to flow through, with grace and the power to create anything. I can see examples of peace in the world, yet my driving force is the peace within my heart. It is this foundation in my life. Where one finds this level of inspiration, all factors are erased. This is the inspiration of spirit inside of you. I often refer to inspiration as *in-spirits-action*. There is a driving force within all of us that, when sparked like a forest fire, will burn all things away to continue to reach its destruction. Look around you, and see what it is that inspires you about the world, and what in it can allow you to look into and continue to elevate you to the highest? What is it you want? Under that is a root, a root that can stand for all moments. Catch this wave and allow it to flow you along all moments.

Open up to confidence within. One who is confident in his or her own abilities will find an unshakeable space to continue to move forward. One who is confident in themselves will continue to reach far. Confidence is a huge factor in the space a warrior holds. It allows for success in many ways. The team that has the most players who are confident in the final outcome will win the game. We can see this currently in the NFL. Occasionally, there are players who have elevated their skills beyond those of others, but in this team atmosphere, the overall talent is virtually the same. The mental agreements we make hold us up in the end. Through confidence, we are showing we have made the agreement that we will win. The ability to lead stands strong within every successful team. We find that every warrior in a tribe, or a player on a team, must cultivate this characteristic within. By possessing the trait of leadership within oneself, we see and understand the ability to follow. Within every phase of life, we have to be able to follow. By following, we eventually find that we are in the flow with spirit. A great leader sees how to stand for others and lifts everyone up together. A player may grow to be the captain, and at times they follow the coach; the coach may follow the owner; the owner may follow the commissioner; and so on, through many layers above and below. It is through following that we embrace and understand the ability to lead.

In the end, a leader knows where they fit in the overall picture of all things. They see how they are in existence with everyone. They understand how they fit in the big picture. A leader is a person who leads by example for the highest good of everyone involved. It is time for all to see, in any moment, that they are leading. Where are you leading everyone around you to?

Turn to cultivate the "Champion Warrior" in you. The "Warrior" is one who has the discipline to execute what is needed, in order to land in self-mastery. No matter what your trade is, take the time to perfect it. The key is to be disciplined and find mastery in your trade. No matter what position you are, what you do, or where you are going, discipline is the key here. Discipline is going to keep us on track. We have all had those resolutions at the beginning of the year, and we fall off: the letting go of coffee, giving up sugar, the gym, and more. It will take discipline to reach ten thousand hours to open up to the mastery of where you are going. A tripod has three legs and is designed to stand on any surface, even if one part is higher than another. It is able to stay balanced to hold up in any moment. Mastery is like the tripod. Once you have put in the time, commit again to ten thousand hours at what you desire. The master will be able to stand on any surface and hold a powerful position.

There are three legs of mastery that any Warrior will reach on their way to ultimate success. The first is to know one's self. To understand how your patterns have held you back from your full power. In this knowing, one gains access to his or her highest self. The second leg of mastery for any Warrior is to stay open, and be with anything and anyone that comes into your life, allowing acceptance to enter each moment, letting go of any need to be attached or pushing away in any way. The third and final leg of mastery for any Warrior is mastery of empowering those around them, sharing knowledge and wisdom to help others reach their highest. By releasing this level of focus, we are able to step up and help all shift into connection of spirit and access greatness.

The Champion Warrior mentality is a trait where those who access the spirit of the game walk with purpose in all aspects of their life. A Champion Warrior mentality is opened to seeing the truth in all, and when we strip it all down, we are able to live and create our reality. A champion has taken the time to dissect the operations of an open mind. In this dissection, a Champion Warrior has undergone their own surgery of their personal mode of operation. This mode has been understood as the Champion Warrior grasping the understanding that their game is 80 percent mental and 20 percent physical. In their understanding, a Champion Warrior has seen that their results are a direct response to how they are seeing the world through their eyes. The Champion Warrior understands that at any moment, the way a moment takes place within their mind field will determine the action they take, shaping their character as viewed by others, ultimately leading to the final result.

Another trait of a Champion Warrior is living the "Warrior's way." Ultimately, we all can relate to the ease in getting something going. The Warrior's way is a lifestyle that refers to one understanding their ultimate desire to bring forward peace, love, and community. Take the time to ask yourself: what is it you want? Be willing to ask this question until it is clear. You will then align yourself to your true desires. At the core of it all, we all want, peace, love, and community.

We often say we want one thing, and our actions reflect that we want something quite the opposite. It is important to get clear and take ownership of what you are truly reaching for. Is your language supporting what you desire? Often players say they want to be the best. Yet, when practice ends, who is left on the field studying plays, visiting with the coach, getting sleep, and putting in the time to align with their desire? The Warrior's way sees the end result of every action. They call themselves into action to support where they desire to go. The Warrior's way is our alignment in all facets of life, to reach deep within for your desire. You will see that, in time, all things come to be when you have reached for your true desire.

A trait of a Champion Warrior that truly has the ability to see clearly is that they will continually fall back on the attitude of gratitude. The Warrior who can find the greatness in all moments is the one who will attract more of the same. The Warrior who finds gratitude opens the door for shifts on the inside. The shifts on the inside lead to healing, a new view in mindset, and a way to bring the best forward in every situation. The practice of gratitude is contagious and allows others to join in and lift each other up to their highest.

The final trait of the Champion Warrior is integrity. Integrity stands for a code that the ELITE live in. There is a state of being that is whole in every moment, allowing the Champion Warrior of life to stand strong, rooted from a solid foundation. It is within this state that all parts of the game come together and champions are found. Take a moment and evaluate a team; a team has many different pieces to it: coaches, players, managers, owners, trainers, and more. It is important for the team to find a common objective and align to it. Take a moment, and look at the team like a bicycle. The objective of the bicycle is to move from point A to point B. In order for the bicycle to move, a rider is involved. The rider gets on and pedals the bike to make the tires move, and with the help of the frame, the bike will reach its destination. Yet if we break it down further, we can see that each part must have integrity to perform. The wheel has spokes; if spokes were missing, the bike would collapse. As with the bicycle, the Champion Warrior finds integrity that carries them through all bases of the game. They find that, ultimately, their integrity arises from use of their words. It is through their words that they become aware of their actions. Through their actions, they find that their results align with where they desire to be. Ultimately, the ELITE understands that the deep root starts with their thoughts. To be ELITE, you gain access to love. Every Loving Individual Trusting Excellence. It is time for you to be ELITE in every way.

CHAPTER 5
The Universal Game of Life

When we look at the universal game of life, we begin to understand the spirit that runs through all that comes up. We must first realize the patterns that we are running, how our operating systems are running a cycle. The cycle we are referring to is known as the game plan. There are things that happen, facts that are almost undeniable. We sit in a place as the observer of these facts. As we observe these facts consciously, or unconsciously, we will find that there is a vibration that comes from each interaction with the fact. These vibrations start out as our thoughts. Through our thoughts, we create a story, and in that story, we've become the main character of each scene.

Once we have created a story around the facts, another vibration is then sent out. This vibration is known as our feeling. Our feelings begin to pulse out into the world and act like magnets, pulling to us the next creation in our reality. This continues as the cycle, around and around we go. Until we see that we have created the cycles of our life, we will continue to live them. Once we have broken the cycle, we have an opportunity to move forward in the way that we desire. So often, it is in this game plan that people get stuck, stuck in the patterns of old, living out the past as it becomes our present moment, ultimately continuing to bring forward the future that we have known in the past.

Once we open up to a new place, we start to understand that we have the ability to attract to us a new future that becomes our present moment. When we are in this moment, right here and now, our past becomes a new moment. It is up to each of us to create from a space of the unknown, to create a new place, to create a new future.

One place that we are stuck in our lives is in the defensive posture we acquire based on our past experiences. We have often gone through some particular moment in our past that triggers us to identify new moments from the perspective of our past hurt. When we identify with our past in this way, our body takes on a defensive posture. We may stand with our arms crossed, walk around with a scowl on our face, or clench our jaw, from what is often known as a fight response in our body. Once we begin to recognize our defensive posture, we can then begin to move forward and live from the new place.

At four years old, I really didn't enjoy eating, often not wanting to eat my food. There were times my dad would get me to eat out of fear of me being too thin. I wanted to stand up for myself. In that moment, I wasn't strong enough to do that. So I created this space within me. This space would establish a need to be right in every way. It would carry through my life in moments that I would defend myself, even if I knew there might be another way. It was in the cycle of my defensive posture that I had this desire to protect me. Once I realized that I had lived from that space, I was able to move forward and listen to others and trust myself to know what would work for me. I was open to another way of being, the better way for me.

Another place we get stuck in our lives is with our offensive posture, which also has been built around fear. The fear that arose from past moments that continues to play out, unless we create a new place for us to live from. We take this offensive posture, a form of attack, in order to take control of the outcome at hand. In most cases, we have developed our strongest characteristics based on a lack of what we could have been in a given moment. We create these offensive postures in order to protect ourselves from the fear of not being enough. Once we become aware of these fears, we do not have to shift our way of being, as there is no reason to get rid of our strongest qualities. By simply being aware that we often use these qualities as fear of not being enough, we will allow ourselves the space to open up to the fullness that love can create around these qualities.

There are a few moments that echoed through my life, from the space of my offensive posture. The first again was the four-year-old who wanted to be protected and wanted to be right. I created this need to be right because I knew the truth for myself. It grew into a place of when someone looked like they knew, I would have to shoot them down immediately, in order to remain protected in my righteousness. As I got older, I was able to recognize that I was living from this place of fear, and once it was released, I actually was able to discover that the spaces that I was blindsided with, opened up to a new possibility for myself and created another way to live from a higher place within.

Another moment where I operated in my offensive posture was when I was coaching college football. I was twenty-four years old when I would get my first full-time job, one of the youngest ever in Division-1 college football. Every Division-1 football team had to hire two minority coaches on every staff. Although there were a number of applicants, I believed that I could have been a token hire. I recall my interview with coach Novak, when he told me if I had any questions, to wait to ask him at the end of the interview. I felt as though I had interviewed poorly because I never really got to show him what I knew it was to be a coach. He had a whiteboard there I wanted to use to be able to draw him some plays, and I never got the chance. So I wasn't sure how the interview really went. In that moment, I also figured I wasn't old enough to get the job. In that moment, I knew I had to become a much stronger leader than I showed myself to be on this interview. I can recall now, looking back, that I knew and paid attention to football so much that I knew a lot about the game, and there was so much more I would've learned had I not had the chip on my shoulder of needing to be the leader to keep my job. Ultimately, I am still a leader today; it just comes from a different space. It comes from a space of love for myself and love for everyone that I am interacting with and leading. It gives me the space to help others become great leaders, as opposed to being fearful they may leave me in order to lead. This new awareness has allowed the growth of my staff to accelerate well beyond the growth we had in the past.

When we have gained access to seeing ourselves, we can let go of the need to be perceived as good or bad. We can let go of the need to avoid judgments of others based on ourselves. We now can let go and move forward from being all about ourselves, to being generously available for others. Once we recognize that we have lived from a place of our past perceptions, we will then understand that we have the ability to live from love in every way.

Now that we have recognized the cycles we live in and begin to understand further where we throw up a guard to live with our defensive posture, and to move forward from the fear of our offensive posture, we then can begin to understand how being for others will attract the special teams we have been looking for. When we open up to our fullest selves, we open up to drawing support and being support for others from our highest vibration.

CHAPTER 6
Nahi Warrior Wisdom

*When a Nahi Warrior dives into the **I am**, what remains is wisdom.*

1. Love is love. When we have reasons or conditions around our expression of love, a Warrior knows that they have yet to be love for another. In order to be love for the world, we must move into unconditional love, which is truly all love without conditions.
2. By removing the conditions, a Warrior will have access to everything, experience freedom, mankind will change, and ultimately birth something new.
3. All need self-love; for a Warrior to gain a new operating system, they must be willing to un-teach themselves what has been taught. As a Warrior untangles the web that has been woven, a Warrior will know we are one.
4. A Warrior is willing to spread the word, which everyone needs to know, that everyone is connected. Go and share; the more you give, the more it will all be revealed.
5. A Warrior knows there won't be peace until all have peace—a simple fact and a wise understanding.
6. A Warrior knows that the way he or she speaks to spirit will bring forward what is asked. Ask for it, present the questions, and allow them to be revealed.

7. A Warrior knows to give more space to be okay. When a Warrior is searching they must land, be, and receive.
8. A Warrior knows that they must do the work. Enter into all phases and allow it all to move forward.
9. A Warrior is willing to be the reflection and allow others to know who they are, and know it to be true.
10. A Warrior is willing to take several deep breaths a day, 54 or 108. I breathe, therefore I am.

Mind Field Meditation System is a twenty-one day meditation to help you establish a solid foundation in your meditation practice. This may also serve as your future daily meditation practice. Your first step will be to begin to establish your meditation area. As you set up your meditation area, first gather a few items to help you build the energy of the space. You will need five items that represent each element in the world. A candle represents the first element, fire; something to hold water for the second element; the third element of air can be represented by a bell or a feather; and dirt, bone, sand, or stone for the fourth element. If you have a picture that will represent spirit for you, this would complete the fifth and final element. You can use these elements to build an altar or create a sacred circle to sit and meditate in. You're building an interaction between you and these elements. You will find that as the elements in you come to balance, the same will take place with the elements on the outside. As you determine where you will sit, choose a place that will have as few disruptions or distractions as possible. I recommend you establish the same time of day to practice daily. Once you establish the space, we will begin this journey of connection. For twenty-one days, we will dive into capturing the present moment. Before each meditation session, establish a comfortable seated position for yourself. Find a space where your spine is straight, with your shoulders back over your hips, and your head in a neutral position. This will create an open channel for energy to pass through your spine. Now we want to bring your mind to a simple inward point.

Twenty-one days: *start with a two-minute meditation morning and/or night; increase your time two minutes every other day.*

day 1, two minutes

day 3-four minutes

day 5-six minutes

day 7-eight minutes

day 9-ten minutes

day 11-twelve minutes

day 13-fourteen minute

day 15-sixteen minutes

day 17-eighteen minutes

day 19-twenty minutes

day 21-twenty to thirty minutes.

Using a timer may be helpful, so that you can let go and connect more deeply.

Our first meditation practice is to become aware of each breath and how it moves throughout. As we begin this practice, we are strictly counting each cycle of our breath. A cycle is known as our inhalation and our exhalation. Pay attention to your body as you sit. When you breathe in, notice how your body expands and lifts up. As you breathe out, notice how your body contracts and goes inward.

Count each full cycle of conscious breathing from one to ten, and repeat. This may seem easy; just continue to repeat it for a week. If this seems easy, begin to raise the number to from ten to fifteen, twenty, twenty-five, thirty, thirty-five, forty. As you continue through this phase, you will begin to see how the Mind Field Meditation has begun to open up.

Questions to journal for week one are:

1. What body triggers are coming up for you? What are the reactions coming up for you in your body? Where do you feel it in your body?
2. What are the repetitive thoughts coming up?
3. What are your experiences in the morning and night meditation?

I am a human being living the life of my dream.

The Warrior knows there are eight ways that everyone will operate in life. Through living in these eight aspects of living, a Warrior is looking to live in balance in each aspect.

The eight ways of operating in life are spiritual, relationships, belief systems, physical body, earth-self, financial, and community. These are the different aspects that every Warrior moves through from day to day.

My prayer is that as you finish this book and open up to a new awareness of and for yourself, that you have moved beyond that space of fear in your heart, to knowing that you, too, are a child of God and that you are taken care of, just as anyone else is on this planet. You are deserving of the life that you dream of, and it is time for you to live your dream.

I have been blessed to do so many things in my lifetime. I played sports in multiple countries, received a degree from Purdue University, and a master's degree from Eastern Illinois University. I have gone on to coach college football for twelve years with some of the greatest players to ever play the game, and with some of the best coaches to ever coach the game. I've gone on to make music, to create art, and to write books. I am a world healer, a proud father, a gifted son, a loving husband, and who knows what's next?

What I desire by sharing this book is that you now know that the only thing that can hold you back is you. Take a moment, and see what stories you can put behind you, some of them you may share with others to help them move forward in their lives. Others, you may just leave behind, as only lessons to call forward when you need to continue to your highest.

I thank you for taking the time to read this, and may you walk with love. Blessings to you and to everyone that you come in contact with, may they be happy to have met you, and may you be happy to have met them.

Remember to shine bright, there is a star being born inside of you.

Peace and love,
Sid McNairy

Sid McNairy

"Walk with love"

Walk with love
I said I Walk with love
Walk with love
I said I Walk with love
It came to me
From up above
I sat on a Mountain
And looked within
It's in this way
That I live again
There came a time
I live in sin
It was 'cause
I lived with men
In this moment
I found a way
To lift up
So that all will stay
You know within
That there is no sin
You are ready to find the way in
The time to shine not yours or mine
The time is now for all to clear
I woke one morning
It was then
In the mirror
I saw my kin
I set outside

The Warrior Within: A Quest for Peace

The eagle came
He said, son you see me now
Let go, it's just me,
A yogi knows there is a dream
It's in this dream
You know what I mean
There's not much time
To feel the shift
Create space
To open up
When you clear
Have no fear
'Cause you know we all are here
Open up to change the world
It's time to give to the kids again
Walk with love
I said I Walk with love
Walk with love
I said I Walk with love ... Walk with love

THE POWER OF THREE

Three amazing books to take yourself into a deeper practice of understanding it all. Join Sid McNairy and you too can find the warrior within!

YOGA & LIFE EMPOWERMENT

THE WARRIOR WITHIN

NAHI WARRIOR TEACHERS MANUAL

SidMcNairy.com | NahiWellness.com | 4Warriors.com

www.ingramcontent.com/pod-product-compliance
Lightning Source LLC
Chambersburg PA
CBHW021824090426
42811CB00032B/2015/J